NORTH AMERICAN

Gordon Swanborough

# North American

## AN AIRCRAFT ALBUM

No 6

Acro Publishing Company, Inc.

NEW YORK

# Photo Credits

Published by ARCO PUBLISHING
COMPANY, INC.
219 Park Avenue South, New York,
N.Y. 10003

First published 1973

© F. G. Swanborough, 1973

Library of Congress Catalog Card Number
73–78482
ISBN 0–668–03318–5

Printed in Great Britain

*The Aeroplane* 22T
M. J. Axe 106T
Warren M. Bodie 29T, 83
Peter M. Bowers 14, 17T, 39, 40B, 41B, 50T, 56B,
    70T, 80B, 108B
Canadian National Defence Dep 31T, 76T
Crown Copyright 30B, 37T, 52, 53B, 54
J. A. Griffin 21B
Howard Levy 8, 24, 35B, 70B, 71B, 73T, 92, 100B
Martin and Kelman 57B
Harold G. Martin 36B, 57T
T. Matsuzaki 96
Jack McNulty 20, 43T
NASA 101
Stephen P. Peltz 105B, 113B
Pictorial Press 16T
RAAF 38, 78
A. U. Schmidt 66T, 68, 84
Frank Sherteer 22B
E. M. Sommerich 25, 55B, 58T
Lawrence S. Smalley 85B
Sud Aviation 86T
US Air Force 36T, 86B
US Navy 81B, 82
Hugh J. T. Young 23B, 37B, 40T

# Contents

# Introduction

The trend towards a very few large aero-space companies, created through a process of acquisition and merger, is often regarded as a European phenomenon of the 'sixties. However, the first big round of consolidation occurred thirty years earlier in America, where the historic pattern of other industries made such moves inevitable in aircraft manufacturing as soon as it reached maturity. This situation was reached in 1928 and of the several conglomorates then formed, North American Aviation was destined to survive as the most successful, becoming eventually one of the world's largest aircraft companies.

The late 'twenties were the years of the great boom in American business, coinciding with whole-hearted public acceptance of flying and resulting in an eagerness on Wall Street to take a financial stake in what could only be regarded as a growth industry. The boom was destined to be short-lived and when the bubble burst, the aircraft companies suffered along with the others, but the conglomerates were mostly able to survive thanks to their large resources.

Because of its origins, North American Aviation Inc (NAA) is almost unique among the major aircraft companies in that it does not bear the name of a pioneer designer around whose products the company was first formed. Indeed, for the

first six years of its existence, NAA was only a holding company, all its activities being conducted in the name of one or other of its subsidiaries. These, at the time of incorporation on December 6th, 1928, included Curtiss Aeroplane and Motor Company, Wright Aeronautical, Curtiss-Robertson Airplane Manufacturing Company, Curtiss-Caproni Corporation, Travel Air, Moth Aircraft Corporation and Keystone Aircraft Corporation. All these companies had been brought together in August 1929 under the title of Curtiss-Wright Corporation by Clement M. Keys, Canadian born and one-time editor of *The Wall Street Journal*, and it was Keys who launched NAA as the new holding company for this group of companies, in which two million shares were quickly taken up for $25million.

In the next few years, a series of deals resulted in NAA acquiring complete or partial control of other companies, either temporarily or permanently. On January 14th, 1929, The Sperry Gyroscope Co, Inc, was acquired outright, and in June the same year, Pitcairn Aviation Inc was acquired, being reorganised in January 1930 as Eastern Air Transport. Also purchased were Ford Instrument Co and Berliner-Joyce Aircraft Corp, which was renamed B/J Aircraft Corp.

For a time, NAA also had a large stake in Intercontinent Aviation Inc, which founded the Cuban airline Cubana and owned the controlling interest in Cia Aviacion Faucett in Peru and in China Airways Federal Inc. Eastern Air Transport purchased New York Airways in 1931 so this also became an NAA company, and another deal brought in a 47½ per cent

interest in Transcontinental & Western Air (the original TWA). On the manufacturing side, a stake was acquired temporarily in Douglas Aircraft Co Inc at Santa Monica.

Major reorganisation of the North American empire began in 1933, including a deal with General Motors Corp which ended up with a 29 per cent share of the parent company. General Motors had previously taken over the Fokker Aircraft Corporation (itself a merger of Atlantic Aircraft Corp and Dayton-Wright Company) and had set up General Aviation Corporation to consolidate its aircraft manufacturing activities. In addition, it had a 47½ per cent interest in TWA, like North American, and a substantial stake in Western Air Express.

To rationalise these various holdings, North American set up The Sperry Corporation to acquire all the NAA holdings in Sperry, Ford Instrument, Intercontinent Aviation and Curtiss-Wright Corporation. These companies thus ceased to be directly controlled by the North American board of directors. On the manufacturing side, B/J Aircraft Corp was merged with General Aviation as the General Aviation Manufacturing Corporation and work was concentrated in the former Curtiss-Caproni factory at Dundalk, Maryland. Ernest R. Breech of General Motors became president of North American and of Eastern, with operation of the latter becoming a General Motors responsibility.

The Air Mail Act of 1934 forced a further vital step in the evolution of North American as a manufacturing company by requiring the separation of manufacturing and operating activities. TWA and Eastern were hived off, and in December 1934

Breech offered presidency of NAA to James H. 'Dutch' Kindelberger with the express purpose of turning the company into a major design and production centre, using its own name. Kindelberger, whose influence on North American was to be profound, had learned to fly with the Army Air Service late in World War I after spending a year at the Carnegie Institute of Technology. After leaving the Army, he joined Glenn L. Martin as designer and chief draughtsman until 1925, when he became chief engineer for Donald Douglas, who had left Martin to set up his own company.

Kindelberger accepted Breech's offer and brought with him as chief engineer John Leland Atwood, another Douglas engineer. They stayed together at the head of North American's affairs until Kindelberger's death in 1962, and to these two more than any other individuals, the company owed its reputation for outstanding engineering quality. Kindelberger became board chairman in 1948 when General Motors' Henry M. Hogan retired, Atwood succeeding him as president, and becoming board chairman when Kindelberger died.

General Aviation was renamed the Manufacturing Division of North American which, upon its inception as an aircraft manufacturer in 1934, had 75 employees. General Aviation had produced small quantities of several designs at Dundalk and at the time of Kindelberger's arrival had built the prototype of a military observation aircraft that would go into production eventually as the North American O-47. The new management decided to concentrate its resources on military aircraft, starting with a design for a basic

trainer to meet a specific Army Air Corps requirement. The observation prototype being General Aviation's GA–15, the new trainer was designated NA–16, becoming the progenitor of one of the most famous of all North American aircraft types and one on which the company was able to found its fortunes. Certain earlier General Aviation types, including the GA–43 transport and the PJ–1 flying boats, also became known as North American types.

With an Army contract for the NA–16 secured after prototype evaluation at Wright Field in April 1935, Kindelberger sought new premises where it could be built, turning not unnaturally towards the Los Angeles area which he had come to know and appreciate while working for Douglas at Santa Monica. A suitable site was found at Inglewood, close to Mines Field (now absorbed into Los Angeles International Airport) for a modest rent of $600 a year, and operations began there in January 1936. The new factory was one of the first to be purpose-built for the pro-

duction of modern aircraft, covering an area of 159,000sq ft and with a payroll of 150. To supplement work on the NA–16 variants and the O–47, US Navy contracts were obtained to build floats for Curtiss Seagull seaplanes.

In concentrating upon military aircraft, Kindelberger and Atwood had accurately assessed the market, for re-armament programmes were gaining momentum in many countries. The next few years were to see the introduction of the Mustang and the Mitchell which, with the NA–16 derivatives including the Texan and Harvard, were to make a significant contribution to the effectiveness of Allied air power throughout World War II. Production facilities expanded rapidly under the impetus of wartime demands, not only at Inglewood but at new premises established at Dallas, Texas, and in a government-owned plant operated by North American at Kansas City.

From January 1939 to September 1945, North American built 15,603 Mustangs,

*Built for the US Coast Guard by General Aviation Corporation when the latter was a subsidiary of North American, this air-sea rescue flying-boat was later designated as a North American type by the US Navy, becoming the PJ–1.*

8

9,817 Mitchells and over 15,000 Texan variants. The company also built 966 four-engined Liberators at Kansas City, and three Fairchild C–82s. Contracts for additional quantities of both these types and for 1,000 Lockheed P–80 jet fighters were in hand when V–J Day brought an overnight cancellation of more than 90 per cent of the work in hand. A war-time peak employment of 91,000 had been reached, but the cancellation of contracts for nearly 8,000 aircraft within 24 hours of the war's end rapidly reduced the payroll to below 5,000.

In common with other aircraft manufacturers, North American had to struggle just to stay in existence, but unlike most others it had no experience of producing civil aircraft upon which, it seemed, future prosperity was to depend. An attempt to enter this field with the four-seat Navion proved financially disastrous although the sale of over 1,000 within a year and the subsequent production of even larger numbers by Ryan proved the soundness of the design. Salvation, for North American, lay with the advent of jet propulsion and in diversification into new fields—guided missiles, avionics, rocket engines and nuclear energy. Before the corner was turned, however, General Motors decided that continued investment in aviation was inappropriate, and disposed of its holding in North American in 1948.

Combining jet propulsion and swept wings, North American produced the F–86 Sabre, first supersonic fighter for the USAF, and the company also demonstrated its technological lead by producing the nation's first jet bomber to enter service, the B–45. The Sabre was followed by the

The F–100C Super Sabre assembly line at Los Angeles.

Super Sabre, used by Col Horace A. Hanes in 1955 to set the world's first supersonic speed record. The Super Sabre became widely used by NATO and other air forces, and the importance of its development was recognised by the award to North American of the Collier Trophy.

Late in 1950, production facilities began to expand, and the company took over the government-owned plant at Columbus, Ohio, previously occupied by Curtiss. This plant was devoted almost wholly to the production of aircraft for the US Navy, including the Savage, Fury, Buckeye, Vigilante and Bronco. The success of the Sabre and other programmes helped to expand the payroll by 1954 to 55,000, its highest level for ten years. A new company structure established separate aircraft divi-

sions at Los Angeles and Columbus, and four new divisions—Atomics International, Rocketdyne, Missile Development (later renamed Space and Information Systems) and Autonetics—during 1957, and another, the Science Center, was established in 1962.

A major effort in the missile field was development of the Navaho intercontinental weapon system for the USAF, and although this was cancelled in July 1957 after ten years work, it allowed the company to gain skills in liquid-propellant rocket engines, inertial guidance, supersonic aerodynamics and other technologies that were to be put to good use in other programmes. By the time the Navaho was cancelled, the company was already at work on the XB–70 supersonic bomber and the X–15 research aircraft, two of the most

Above: *North American entered the guided weapon field with the SM–64 Navaho strategic missile—virtually an unmanned supersonic bomber. Development was cancelled after 10 years work.*

Below: *With the NAC–60 design, North American was one of three manufacturers participating in the initial design competition for the US supersonic transport.*

remarkable of all North American aeroplanes.

The Rocketdyne Division became responsible for the engines of many of America's space probes and satellites, including the first satellite, Explorer I. Contributions to the lunar exploration programme included Rocketdyne engines for two stages of the Saturn launch vehicle and the re-entry control system for the Apollo spacecraft, while the spacecraft itself was a product of the Space and Information Systems Division (later renamed the Space Division). These activities and those of the other divisions in space and non-aviation fields resulted in a decline in the relative importance of aircraft production during the 'sixties, a trend which was also hastened by the company's continuing lack of commercial aircraft.

A small but successful venture into the civil field began in 1962 with the Sabreliner, an executive jet version of the T–39, produced originally as a USAF utility trainer and transport. Other civil projects were studied in depth, including the NAC–60 supersonic transport in 1963/64 which made use of XB–70 technology and the NAC–100 Centuryliner in 1964, a twin-jet short haul transport. The breakthrough into the civil field came, however, not from a new aircraft design but through the merger in 1967 with the Rockwell-Standard Corporation. Effected on September 22nd, 1967, this merger produced the North American Rockwell Corporation, with J. L. Atwood continuing as president and chief executive officer, while Willard Rockwell Jr became chairman. Among the Rockwell assets was the Aero Commander Division, in production with

**Above:** *To study possible applications of the Rogallo inflatable wing, North American tested this simulated Gemini space capsule beneath such a wing in 1964.*

**Below:** *In late 1972, NR Columbus won a US Navy contract to build two prototypes of this NR-356 V/STOL fighter/attack aircraft, powered by a Pratt and Whitney F401 turbofan.*

a range of business, light and agricultural aircraft.

Of the Aero Commander types, one—the Jet Commander—could not be made part of the deal since it was a direct competitor of the North American Sabreliner and acquisition would have offended US Anti-Trust laws. The design rights, production tooling and inventory were sold to Israel Aircraft Industries by Rockwell in a separate deal before the merger. Other Aero Commander types, comprising piston and turboprop twins, piston-engined light-planes and a series of agricultural aircraft, were continued in production by North American Rockwell during an interim period of rationalisation which in the course of five years from the merger date eliminated several of these types.

John L. Atwood relinquished his presidency of the company at the end of 1969—marking the end of an era in the company's history—and was replaced by Robert Anderson as president and chief operating officer, while Willard Rockwell became chief executive officer as well as chairman. Major reorganisation in 1971 resulted in the grouping of NR activities under four principal headings: Aerospace Group, Industrial Products Group, Automotive Divisions Group and Electronics Group. The first two of these four were concerned with aircraft production in addition to other activities.

Within the Aerospace Group, aircraft production was being undertaken during 1972 by the Los Angeles Division and the Columbus Aircraft Division; this group also embraced the Autonetics Division, Atomics International Division, Missile System Division, Rocketdyne Division,

Space Division, Tulsa Division and Science Center. The Industrial Products Group included aircraft production under the General Aviation Divisions, embracing the Sabreliner Division at El Segundo (Los Angeles), and the Aero Commander Division with production lines at Bethany, Oklahoma; Albany, Georgia and Los Angeles.

During 1972, the General Aviation Divisions began customer deliveries of a new series of single-engined lightplanes—the first original North American designs for more than a decade—and by March 1972, these divisions had produced a total of 3,548 aircraft. On the military side, the Columbus Division was still producing aircraft for the US Navy and export, while the Los Angeles Division was committed to development of the B-1 supersonic bomber—perhaps the most challenging of all the North American aircraft projects to date and one which, if ordered by the USAF, was destined to keep the name of North American in the forefront of military aircraft manufacturers for years to come.

## Author's Note

The aircraft descriptions that make up the main part of this work are arranged broadly in chronological order, taking as a guide the earliest NA charge number applicable to each design or group of designs. In some cases—notably the NA-16 family of derivatives—it is logical to group a number of aircraft under a single heading, and chronology inevitably suffers somewhat. Also, as a general rule, the NA numbers applicable to derivatives of a

basic design have been excluded from the text.

All available details of NA numbers to date, subject to the provisions of company or national security, are quoted in the type and production list at the end of the book. This listing also indicates the company construction numbers applied to airframes at the time of manufacture. Up to the NA-156, these numbers followed a continuous sequence, with a prefix indicating the charge number. Starting with the NA-157, the system changed to one in which the c/ns started at 1 for each subsequent charge number.

In the production lists that accompany each aircraft description, an attempt is made to list the identity markings in which the aircraft were first delivered. In a number of cases, notably some of the AT-6 and AT-16 contracts, the same aircraft were allocated two or even three series of numbers at the contractual stage, and this explains why some batches of USAAF, USN or RAF numbers are not listed. It is also impossible, in a volume of this size, to list the individual identities of the more recent civil aircraft built in large quantities.

A work of this kind depends in its preparation upon the generous assistance of many individuals. The author gratefully acknowledges the particular contributions, in photographs or information, of Peter M. Bowers, Jack McNulty, John Griffin, John W. R. Taylor, Joe Mizrahi and Pilot Press Ltd. The North American Rockwell Corporation, looking more to the future than the past, finds little time to give to historical research in its own files; the help extended, within these limits, is also acknowledged.

## North American Model Numbers

Since the company began design and production of aeroplanes in its own name at the start of 1935, all North American designs have been identified by 'NA' numbers. These are not, strictly speaking, type or model numbers but are 'charge numbers' used for accountancy and contractual purposes.

Consequently, new NA charge numbers are assigned at various phases of progress with each individual design, for each new contract in the case of production types and for such items as a flight test programme or the preparation of training, technical services and publications. In the aircraft descriptions in this volume, only the NA numbers applicable to basic designs, or those widely used to identify variants (in particular of the NA-16 family) have been quoted. A complete list of the NA charge numbers is included as an appendix, subject to omissions for company commercial and security reasons.

The first NA number used by North American was 16. This was a logical continuation from GA-15, the type number of the experimental Army observation monoplane which was the last type built at Dundalk by General Aviation before the name was changed to North American. When the GA-15 was put into production at North American's new plant at Los Angeles, it was assigned the charge number NA-25. The NA prefix was changed to NR in 1971 following the North American-Rockwell merger. To date, charge numbers have not been applied to the aircraft types produced by the General Aviation Divisions.

# Aeroplane Types

## O–47

The General Aviation GA–15 was designed to provide the US Army Air Corps with a new generation of observation aircraft, improving radically on the performance and capability of the high-wing, open cockpit monoplanes that had been the norm for observation types since World War I. To match the standards being achieved by the new bombers and fighters, the Army specified that its new observation craft should be of all-metal construction, with a max speed over 200mph, service ceiling over 20,000ft, range of at least 700miles, crew of three and defensive armament. These features were provided in the GA–15 design, which had a mid-wing, an 850hp Wright R–1820–41 Cyclone engine and crew of three in tandem beneath a long 'glasshouse' enclosure. For visual observation, an additional crew position was built into the deep fuselage beneath the wing, with front, side and ventral windows; this position was accessible from the centre cockpit, while the third crewman in the rear of the cockpit manned the flexibly-mounted 0·30in gun for rear defence. A similar gun in the wing was fixed to fire forwards and aimed by the pilot.

Completed in the early summer of 1935, the prototype GA–15 was tested at Wright Field in Air Corps markings but with civil registration X–2079; its purchase as the XO–47 was confirmed in January 1936. A production contract for 109 O–47As was approved on February 19th, 1937, and these aircraft began to appear from the Inglewood plant later that year, followed by 55 more on a second contract dated October 20th, 1937. The O–47As had 975hp R–1820–49 engines and most were delivered in natural metal finish; 48 of the second batch were procured for the Air National Guard. Production was completed with 74 O–47Bs, including 24 for the ANG, with 1,060hp R–1820–57s, an increase of

*The prototype XO–47 with original observer's station in the belly.*

*North American O–47B in overall drab finish adopted in 1940.*

50 US gal in internal fuel capacity and higher gross weight. Most O–47As and O–47Bs had revised lower fuselage lines, with less transparencies for the observer.

The O–47s were well distributed through the observation squadrons by 1941, but saw little operational service after America entered the War. A few were used from overseas bases after the Japanese attack on Pearl Harbor, and for a few months in early 1942, some submarine patrols were flown off the US coasts. Thereafter, the O–47s were relegated to training, target-towing and other utilitarian duties. A few O–47Bs survived the war and were modified for commercial use on restricted category certificates, issued on August 1st, 1945. In this rôle, they operated as single seaters with the centre and rear seats removed and cargo tie-downs fitted instead.

### Specification (O–47A)

| | |
|---|---|
| SPAN | 46ft 4in |
| LENGTH | 33ft 7in |
| HEIGHT | 12ft 2in |
| WING AREA | 350sq ft |
| GROSS WEIGHT | 7,636lb |
| MAX SPEED | 221mph |
| CRUISING SPEED | 200mph |
| RANGE | 400 miles |

### Production

*XO–47:* NA–15 NX2079 (36–145).

*O–47A:* NA–25 37–260/368; NA–60 38–271/325.

*O–47B:* NA–51 39–065/138.

# NA–16 family (Fixed undercarriage versions)

## Yale

The last prototype built in the General Aviation plant at Dundalk, Maryland, emerged as the NA–16, a basic trainer to Air Corps requirements and sire of an enormous family of related designs which placed North American firmly on the map. Over 17,000 examples of the various derivatives of the NA–16 were built in North American's Los Angeles and Dallas plants in the next ten years or so, and over 4,500 more were built under licence in four other countries. As the AT–6 Texan or Harvard, a derivative of the basic NA–16 was used as an advanced pilot trainer in America, Britain and several other Allied countries throughout the war, and subsequently became almost as widely known and used throughout the world as the Douglas C–47 Dakota.

The NA–16 as first flown was an all-metal (with partial fabric covering) low-wing monoplane with open cockpits in tandem, a fixed, unfaired undercarriage and a cowled 400hp Wright R–975 Whirlwind radial engine. With the civil registration X–2080, it first flew at Dundalk in April 1935 and was submitted in the Army Air Corps contest for evaluation at Wright Field in the same month. The design was selected for production as a basic trainer, although the Air Corps requested several modifications including an enclosure over the cockpits. The prototype was modified, as NA–18, to have this feature plus faired u/c legs and a 600hp Pratt & Whitney R–1340 engine, in which guise it was

*The prototype of the North American NA–16 series, X–2080, after modification as the NA–18 with enclosed cockpits and other changes, in which form it was sold to Argentina.*

eventually sold to Argentina. Other modifications introduced on various later models included a retractable undercarriage (these versions are described separately), changes in the wing tip and tail unit shape, changes in engine installation and introduction of armament.

In all, 63 different NA charge numbers were applied to members of the NA–16 family, including those built for the US Army Air Corps/Air Force, US Navy and for export. Most of these variants were intended primarily as trainers, but they also included single-seat fighters (NA–50, NA–68) and two-seat light bombers (NA–44, NA–69, NA–72, NA–74) which are described separately. Many of the trainer variants also carried, or had provision for, guns and bombs.

The trainer variants can best be considered in groups according to their customer and in sequence of NA charge numbers, which indicate the order in which the variants were put into development and production. The first group to be considered comprises the fixed undercarriage types for the US Army Air Corps and US Navy, as follows:

*NA–19:* BT–9 basic trainer for AAC, similar to NA–18 with R–975–7 Whirlwind

*Top right: A BT–9 (NA–19) in the 1940 blue and yellow colours of the Army Air Corps, flying over Randolph Field, Texas. Fixed leading edge slats, shown here, were an optional feature.*

*Right: The temporarily modified ninth production BT–9 as a primary trainer (NA–22) with open cockpits.*

engine. First flown in April 1936; 42 built at Inglewood.

*NA–19A:* BT–9A for Air Corps Reserve, as BT–9 with addition of one fixed forward gun firing through propeller arc, and recording camera, and one flexibly-mounted gun in rear cockpit beneath redesigned enclosure; 40 built.

*NA–22:* The ninth NA–19 completed as a primary trainer with open cockpits to meet requirements of Army Circular Proposal 36–28. Modified back to BT–9 standard and delivered as serial 36–36 later.

*NA–23:* BT–9B, as BT–9 with minor changes; 117 built for Air Corps.

*NA–28:* NJ–1, similar to BT–9 for US Navy but fitted with 500hp Pratt & Whitney R–1340 Wasp engine; 40 built at Inglewood, with deliveries starting in July 1937. One aircraft (serial 0949) temporarily as NJ–2 with Ranger XV–770–4 inverted-Vee engine.

*NA–29:* BT–9C for Air Corps Reserve, as BT–9B with armament same as BT–9A. Total of 67 ordered, of which the first (serial 37–383) was completed as Y1BT–10 with a 600hp R–1340 Wasp engine and one other was converted to BT–9D with outer wings and tail unit of the later BC–1A type.

*NA–30:* Drawings for Y1BT–10 (See NA–29).

*NA–58:* BT–14 for AAC, with some features of BC–1A including new outer

Top right: *Blunt-tipped wings and a triangular rudder distinguished the BT–14 (NA–58).*

Right: *The NA–31 or NA–16–4M, one of two pattern aircraft supplied to Sweden.*

wing panels, new tail unit and metal-covered rear fuselage. 450hp R–985–25 Wasp Junior engine; 251 built, of which 27 were converted to BT–14A with R–985–11 engine.

The export of NA–16 variants represented a significant part of North American's business between 1935 and 1939. Although many of the export aircraft carried NA–16 designations, they were also covered by separate charge numbers, as follows:

*NA–18:* The original NA–16 prototype X–2080, modified and sold to Argentina.
*NA–20:* Also NA–16–2H. One aircraft similar to NA–19 built as demonstrator for China and subsequently fitted with R–1340 Wasp engine for sale to Honduras.
*NA–31:* Also NA–16–4M. Basic trainer for Sweden, similar to BT–9 with 450hp Wright R–975–E3 engine. One example built at Inglewood and sold to ASJA together with manufacturing licence.
*NA–32:* Also NA–16–1A. The first of two pattern aircraft purchased, together with production rights, by Commonwealth Aircraft Corporation in Australia (see NA–33). Fixed undercarriage and R–1340 Wasp engine, otherwise similar to NA–26. Delivered in mid-1937 and used by RAAF 1938–1940 as serial A20–1.

**Top right:** *One of 30 NA–16–4P (NA–34) armed trainers sold to Argentina.*

**Right:** *The second NA–57, before delivery to the Armée de l' Air.*

*An early NA–64 in French markings and bearing US civil registration NX13397.*

*NA–34:* Also NA–16–4P. Basic trainer for Argentina, similar to BT–9 with added radio and armament of two forward firing guns, one flexible gun and bomb racks. Thirty built at Inglewood.

*NA–37:* Also NA–16–4R. Basic trainer for Japan, similar to BT–9 with 450hp Pratt & Whitney R–985–9CG engine and three-blade propeller. One demonstrator (and production rights) sold to Mitsubishi in September 1937 and designated KXA1 by the Japanese Navy (see NA–47 also).

*NA–38:* Also NA–16–4M. One airframe, same as NA–31, supplied to Sweden unassembled.

*NA–41:* Also NA–16–4. Basic trainer for China, similar to BT–9C with Whirlwind engine. Thirty-five built at Inglewood (see NA–48).

*NA–42:* Also NA–16–2A. Two aircraft supplied to Honduras, similar to NA–20 with armament added.

*NA–43:* Also NA–16–1G. Projected version of BT–9C for Brazilian Army Air Force; not built.

*NA–46:* Also NA–16–4. Twelve aircraft supplied to Brazilian Navy in 1939, similar to BT–9C with armament, centre section bomb racks and Whirlwind engine.

*NA–47:* Also NA–16–4RW. One aircraft similar to NA–37 but with Wright R–975–E3 and two-blade propeller, supplied to Japan unassembled in December

1937. Designated KXA2 by Japanese Navy.

*NA–56:* Also NA–16-4. Fifty for China, similar to NA–55/BC–1A with Wasp engine, blunt-tipped wings and new rudder shape, but with fixed undercarriage.

*NA–57:* Basic trainer for France, similar to NA–23 (BT–9B) with fixed undercarriage and Wright R–975 Whirlwind engine. 230 built at Inglewood, including 30 for Aéronavale. Operated by Armée de l'Air in Et2 (Entrainement biplace) and P2 (Perfectionnement biplace) categories. Some captured and used by Luftwaffe.

*NA–64:* Similar to NA–57 for France, with revised wing and tail unit as introduced on NA–55. Contracts for 200 for l'Armée de l'Air and 30 for Aéronavale, but only 111 delivered to France (some being captured for use by Luftwaffe); the remainder were taken over by Britain and diverted to the RCAF which used them as Yale Is.

*A Yale (one of 119 NA–64s ordered by France but transferred to the RCAF) serving as a wireless trainer.*

# NA–16 family (Retractable u/c variants)

Harvard, Texan

During 1937, the Air Corps organised a contest for a 'basic combat' aircraft—a new category of trainer intended to have the same armament, equipment and characteristics as operational aircraft. To meet the requirements set out in Army Circular Proposal 37–220, North American built a variant of the NA–16 with a 600hp Pratt & Whitney R–1340 engine, a retractable undercarriage, provision for forward and rear armament and navigation and engine instruments representative of a combat type. This prototype was known as the NA–26 and was the immediate progenitor of the AT–6 Texan and Harvard types; it was eventually sold to Canada as noted later. The group of retractable-gear variants for the USAAC and USN that derived from the NA–26 was as follows:

*NA–36:* BC–1 basic combat trainer for AAC, similar to NA–26 with R–1340–7 engine. Orders totalled 180 of which 30 were equipped for instrument training as BC–1I and the last three became BC–2 (NA–54).

*NA–52:* SNJ–1 scout trainer for USN, similar to BC–1 but with metal-covered rear fuselage and integral centre-section fuel tanks; 16 built in 1939.

*NA–54:* BC–2, last three aircraft on BC–1 contract with R–1340–45 engines, three-bladed propellers, metal-covered rear fuselage, integral fuel tanks, new rudder shape and blunt-tipped wings.

*NA–55:* BC–1A, as • BC–1 with revised, blunt-tipped, outer wing-shape and straight trailing edge to rudder, as first used on the NA–44. Ordered for National Guard (29) and AC Reserve (54). One later became BC–1B when fitted with an AT–6A centre section and nine more ordered as BC–1A were delivered as AT–6 (NA–59).

*NA–59:* AT–6, continuation of BC–1A contract, with change of designation from 'basic combat' to 'advanced trainer' category; total of 94 for AAC including nine originally ordered as NA–55.

*NA–65:* SNJ–2, similar to SNJ–1 with R–1340–56 engine and controllable-pitch propeller; 36 built in 1940.

*NA–77:* AT–6A and SNJ–3 for Army Air Corps and Navy; production totals 517 and 120 respectively, built at Inglewood. Similar to AT–6 with R–1340–9 engine and revised fuel tanks.

*NA–78:* AT–6A and SNJ–3, as NA–77 but built at North American Dallas, Texas, plant—1,330 for AAC and 150 for USN.

*NA–79:* SNJ–2, continuation of NA–65; 25 built on this contract.

*NA–84:* AT–6B, similar to AT–6A with R–1340–AN–1 engine and equipped for gunnery training; 400 built at Dallas.

*NA–85:* Originally allocated to contract for 150 SNJ–3; aircraft built as NA–78s.

*NA–88:* AT–6C and AT–6D, SNJ–4 and SNJ–5, similar to AT–6A but AT–6C/

*Top right: NA–26, first of the series with a retractable undercarriage, in its original form.*

*Right: The NA–26 in service with the RCAF, with the later form of rudder fitted.*

SNJ–4 used non-strategic materials to save 1,250lb of aluminium alloy per aircraft, and AT–6D/SNJ–5 had 24-volt (instead of 12-volt) electric system. Production total 9,331 at Dallas, comprising 2,970 AT–6C, 2,604 AT–6D, 2,400 SNJ–4 and 1,357 SNJ–5. One AT–6D became XAT–6E when fitted with a Ranger V–770–9 engine, and some of the USN aircraft became SNJ–5C when fitted with arrester gear.

*NA–121:* AT–6D (800) and AT–6F (956) built at Texas; 419 more on this contract cancelled. The AT–6F had strengthened wing panels and redesigned rear fuselage, and 931 of the total built were assigned to the Navy as SNJ–6.

*NA–128:* Contract for 1,200 AT–6D, cancelled.

In addition to the AT–6s listed above, the USAAF also assigned the AT–16 designation to the same basic type, built in Canada by Noorduyn (see below) and paid for by lend-lease funds. Under lend-lease arrangements also, some 2,300 AT–6s were supplied to Britain, the Soviet Union, China, Brazil and other nations; those for Britain were known as Harvard IIA (AT–6C) and Harvard III (AT–6D and SNJ–5). The AT category was abandoned by the USAAF in 1948 and more than 2,000 AT–6s then still in service were redesignated T–6A, T–6C, T–6D and T–6F.

Prior to and during World War II, versions of the retractable-undercarriage NA–16 design were exported to several nations, starting with the original NA–26 demonstrator itself, which went to Canada in July 1940, acquiring the RCAF serial 3345 and the new 'angular' fin at the same

time. The subsequent export versions were as follows:

*NA–27:* Also NA–16–2H. European demonstrator based on NA–26 as a basic combat trainer, with retractable undercarriage and R–1340 Wasp engine. The demonstrator was delivered to Fokker in Holland as PH–APG and Fokker also acquired an option to build the NA–16 in Europe. The sole NA–27 entered service with the Dutch Air Force with the serial 997 and was destroyed in a Luftwaffe attack on the base at De Vlijt, Texel on May 11th, 1940.

*NA–33:* Also NA–16–2K. Second pattern aircraft for Australia (see NA–32). Similar to NA–26, with retractable undercarriage. Delivered late-1937 and used by RAAF 1938–1940 as serial A20–2. Produced in Australia as the Wirraway (see below).

*NA–45:* Also NA–16–1GV. Three aircraft supplied to Venezuela, similar to NA–36 (BC–1).

*NA–48:* Also NA–16–3C. Fifteen aircraft for China, similar to NA–36.

*NA–49:* Also NA–16–1E. Harvard I advanced trainer for the RAF, built on British contract. Similar to NA–36 (BC–1) with British-specified equipment. Total of 400 built at Inglewood.

Top left: *Harvard I (NA–49), one of 400 built on British contracts, in early finish with green/ brown upper surfaces and yellow undersides.*

Left: *The US Navy's SNJ–2 (NA–65) showing the retractable undercarriage and original rounded rudder.*

*NA-61:* Also NA-16-1E. Basically similar to NA-49 Harvard I, for RCAF. Thirty delivered.

*NA-66:* Harvard II advanced trainer for RAF and Commonwealth, similar to NA-59 (AT-6) with new rudder and blunt-tipped wings. Total of 600 built—20 delivered to RAF, 67 to RNZAF, 511 assigned to RCAF (but 23 of these not delivered) and two crashed before delivery to RCAF.

*NA-71:* Also NA-16-3. Three aircraft for Venezuela, similar to NA-59 (AT-6).

*NA-75:* Harvard II advanced trainer, same as NA-66. Contract for 100 for RCAF.

*NA-76:* Harvard II advanced trainer, same as NA-66. Original contract for 450 placed by France, all taken over by Britain for RAF and RCAF, the latter receiving 259 of the total.

*NA-81:* Harvard II advanced trainer, same as NA-66. Contract for 125, of which 24 delivered to RAF and 101 to RCAF.

*NA-119:* AT-6Ds for Brazil in 1944: supplied as 10 complete airframes subassembled, 10 partially subassembled and 61 complete airframe sets of parts.

Many nations received T-6s from surplus USAAF, RAF and RCAF stocks in the

*Top right: An AT-6A (NA-77) serving as a gunnery trainer, with flexibly mounted gun in rear cockpit.*

*Right: A Harvard II (NA-81) carrying RAF serial BW206 but operated by the RCAF throughout the war and shown here in post-war markings.*

years following World War II, and these were used for light attack duties as well as for training. For example, the Spanish Air Force used several squadrons of T–6s as single-seat attack aircraft (designated C6), with a fixed armament of two 7·7mm Breda machine guns and underwing provision for 12 Oerlikon air-to-ground rockets or 10 22lb bombs. Similarly, the Brazilian Air Force operated T–6s in the attack rôle into the early 'seventies. In addition, large numbers of surplus T–6s were sold to civilians and were operated on a variety of duties including target-towing and crop spraying by civilian agencies. As a sporting aeroplane, the T–6 became a favourite mount for pilots competing in races in the USA, and its use in this way led to many modifications designed to enhance performance, such as the elimination of one cockpit and the long cockpit enclosure and substitution of a small tear-drop hood, the use of wing-tip tanks, uprated engines and so on. One of the most-modified of all T–6s was the Bacon Super T–6, tested in 1957; this had a one-piece blown canopy, tricycle under-carriage and wing-tip tanks. Other modifications provided for two or three passengers to be carried behind the pilot.

Starting in 1949, the North American company began a remanufacturing programme that eventually embraced 1,812 T–6s, which were redesignated after modification to have revised cockpit layout and seating, increased fuel, revised landing gear and other changes. These conversion programmes carried new NA numbers as listed below; new USAF serial numbers were also assigned. In addition, some USN Texans were updated to SNJ–7 and SNJ–7B

(with armament) at NAS Pensacola in 1952, but were not covered by NA numbers.

*NA–168:* T–6G, remanufactured at Downey. 641 for USAF and 50 for Air National Guard. Also 59 as LT–6G for operation as Forward Air Controllers in Korea.
*NA–182:* T–6G, remanufactured at Columbus. 824 for USAF, including some converted T–6Fs temporarily redesignated T–6H.
*NA–188:* T–6G, remanufactured at Long Beach. 107 for USAF, all assigned to Mutual Defense Aid Programmes.

*NA–195:* T–6G, remanufactured at Fresno. 11 for USAF, assigned to MD Aid.
*NA–197:* T–6G, remanufactured at Fresno, using 110 ANG T–6D airframes.
*NA–198:* A US Navy contract was placed in 1952 for production of 240 SNJ–8s, similar to the T–6G standard; the contract was cancelled with none built.

One other applicable NA charge number was NA–186, which covered the provision of design data to Canadian Car and Foundry for production of the updated T–6 configuration.

*AT–6D (NA–88) serving with the Air Force Reserve, showing post-war markings.*

# NA–16 family (Licence production)

Harvard, Wirraway, Ceres

As indicated in the foregoing accounts, licences for production of NA–16 variants were acquired by the Netherlands, Sweden, Japan, Australia and Canada. No production took place in the Netherlands; details of the other programmes follow:

*Australia:* Production of the NA–33 by Commonwealth Aircraft Corporation was put in hand during 1937, as the first project of the newly-formed company at Fishermen's Bend. The design was adapted to meet RAAF requirements for a general purpose aircraft, with a strengthened fuselage, additional equipment and the usual single gun replaced by two 0·303s in the upper fuselage behind the cowling. Named Wirraway (aborigine for Challenger) and powered by a 600hp Wasp R–1340–S1H1 (also built under licence by Commonwealth Aircraft Corporation), the first Australian-built aircraft flew on March 27th, 1939.

Production totalled 755, of which the last 147 were delivered without armament. Many Wirraways served operationally as fighters and dive bombers in the early wartime period and later as trainers and for communications until 1959. A series of Commonwealth Aircraft Corporation contract numbers was applied to the production batches, comprising CA–1, CA–3, CA–5, CA–7, CA–8, CA–9, CA–10 (a projected bomber version), CA–10A (dive bomber), CA–16 and CA–20 (conversion for Navy use). Post-war, some Wirraways were converted by Common-

*A Navy Texan modified for deck-landing training, with arrester hook, as SNJ–5C (NA–88).*

wealth to CA-28 Ceres as single-seat agricultural aircraft.

*Canada:* Production of a version of the Harvard similar to the AT-6A was put in hand in Canada to meet the rapidly expanding demand for pilot trainers after the outbreak of war and the launching of the British Commonwealth Air Training Program. The manufacturer chosen by the Canadian government was Noorduyn Aviation Ltd in Montreal and a first contract for 100 was placed in January 1940. A second order for 110 followed in July, and these 210 aircraft were delivered to the RCAF as Harvard IIBs. Further Noorduyn production was financed by the US government, which ordered 1,500 for supply to the RAF under Lend-Lease arrangements. These aircraft were assigned the USAAF designation AT-16 (and USAAF serial numbers) but were delivered as Harvard IIBs with RAF serial numbers, many being retained for service in Canada. Production continued with another 900 for the RAF, bringing total Noorduyn production to 2,610, a further 300 on order for the RAF being cancelled.

A second Canadian programme was launched in 1951 when the RCAF ordered a new production batch of Harvards

Top left: *The single XAT-6E, a modified AT-6D (NA-88) with a Ranger in-line engine.*

Left: *An early AT-6 model remanufactured in 1949 as T-6G (NA-168) with improved canopy, new radio equipment and many other changes.*

Right: *An ex-US Navy SNJ-5 operating with the French Aeronavale after the war.*

similar to the modernised T-6G. These went into production at the Canadian Car and Foundry plant in Montreal, this company having taken over Noorduyn in 1946, and they were designated Harvard IV by the RCAF, which acquired 270. A further 285 were purchased from the CCF production line by the USAF with the designation T-6J for use in the Mutual Aid Program. The USAF also received six of the RCAF's Harvard IVs to replace six AT-6Ds lost in a batch of 100 on loan to the RCAF from 1951 to 1954.

*Japan:* After the Japanese Navy had evaluated the KXA1 and KXA2 (see NA-37 and NA-47), production of a modified version was put in hand to meet a Navy requirement for an intermediate trainer. Production was entrusted to KK Watanabe Tekkosho and the first example was completed in 1941; designated K10W1,

it had revised fin and rudder, a 7·7mm Type 97 machine gun and a 600hp Nakajima Kotobuki 2 Kai engine. After 26 had been built, production was transferred at the end of 1942 to Nippon Hikoki KK, which built 150 similar aircraft designated K5Y1 in 1943 and 1944. During the war, these aircraft were assigned the Allied code-name of Oak.

*Sweden:* The licence to build a version of the NA-16 in Sweden was acquired in 1937 by AB Svenska Järnvägsverkstäderna (ASJA), and two specimen airframes were obtained from North American—one NA-31 and one NA-38. These examples had the Wright R-975-E3 Whirlwind engine, and substantially the same type went into production at the ASJA plant against a Swedish Air Force contract for 35 placed in July 1938. These aircraft went into service with the Swedish Air Force

designation SK 14 from May 1939 onwards, and were followed by a second batch of 18 built by Saab (which had absorbed ASJA) at Linkoping in 1940–41.

In the third production batch, ordered from Saab in May 1940, a 500hp Piaggio P VII R.C.35 engine was used and the 23 aircraft in this batch, delivered from August 1941 to June 1942, were identified as Sk 14A. A final order for 60 Sk 14s was placed at the Saab Trollhattan plant in February 1942 and these were delivered between September 1943 and October 1944. During 1944, one Sk 14 was converted to have a fixed nosewheel undercarriage as a test-bed for the Saab J 21.

All the Swedish-built Sk 14s were basic trainers of the BT-9 type, with fixed landing gear, and should not be confused with the retractable-gear Texans purchased by the Swedish Air Force from surplus

*A typically much-modified AT–6 for post-war sporting use, with in-line engine, modified canopy and dorsal fin.*

stocks after the end of the war. These comprised 145 AT–16s designated Sk 16A, 112 T–6s designated Sk 16B and six SNJ–2s designated Sk 16C.

## Specification (NA–16 series)

|  | BT–9 | BC–1 | AT–6A |
|---|---|---|---|
| SPAN | 42ft | 43ft | 42ft |
| LENGTH | 27ft 7in | 27ft 9in | 29ft |
| HEIGHT | 13ft 7in | 14ft | 11ft 9in |
| WING AREA | 248sq ft | 225sq ft | 254sq ft |
| GROSS WEIGHT | 4,470lb | 5,200lb | 5,155lb |
| MAX SPEED | 170mph | 207mph | 210mph |
| CRUISING SPEED | 147mph | | |
| RANGE | 700 miles | 665 miles | 629 miles |

## Production

*NA–16:* X.2080.
*BT–9:* 36–028 to 36–069.
*NJ–1:* 0910 to 0949.
*BT–9A:* 36–088 to 36–127.
*BT–9B:* 37–115 to 37–231.
*BT–9C:* 37–383 to 37–415, 38–224 to 38–257.
*BT–14:* 40–1110 to 40–1360.
*NA–20:* NC 16025.
*NA–26:* 3345 (RCAF).

**Top left:** *Probably the most-modified of the NA–16 family—the Bacon Super T–6 in 1957 with new engine, nosewheel, tip tanks and one-piece canopy.*

**Left:** *Australian-built Wirraway by Commonwealth Aircraft, with early style wing-tips and rudders, plus retractable undercarriage.*

NA–27: R–17377.
NA–31: 671.
NA–32: A20–1.
NA–33: A20–2.
NA–34: 30 for Argentina.
BC–1: 37–416 to 37–456, 37–636 to 37–679, 38–356 to 38–447.
BC–1A: 39–798 to 39–856, 40–707 to 40–716, 40–726 to 40–739.
BC–2: 38–448 to 38–450.
NA–37: One for Japan.
NA–38: One for Japan.
NA–41: 35 for China.
NA–42: Two for Honduras.
NA–45: Three for Venezuela.
NA–46: 12 for Brazil.
NA–47: One for Japan.
NA–48: 15 for China.
NA–56: 50 for China.
NA–71: Three for Venezuela.
Harvard I: N7000 to N7199, P5783 to P5982, 1321 to 1350 (RCAF).
Harvard II: AJ538 to AJ987, BW184 to BW207, AH185 to AH204, 2501 to 3033 (RCAF), 3134 to 3233 (RCAF), 3761 to 3841 (RCAF), NZ901 to NZ967 (RNZAF).
NA–57: Na–57–1 to Na–57–230.
NA–64: Na–64–1 to Na–64–111.

Top left: *The Commonwealth CA–28 Ceres modification of the Wirraway for agricultural use.*

Left: *Last-but-one Noorduyn-built Harvard IIB in all-yellow RAF finish.*

Top right: *Canadian Car and Foundry-built Harvard IV, with features similar to the T–6G.*

Right: *A Swedish-built version of the NA–16, known as Sk 14A to the Swedish Air Force, with Piaggio P VII RC 35 engine.*

*Yale 1:* 3346 to 3464 (RCAF).
*AT-6:* 40-717 to 40-725, 40-2080 to 40-2164.
*AT-6A-NA:* 41-149 to 41-665.
*AT-6A-NT:* 41-666 to 41-785, 41-15824 to 41-17033.*
*AT-6B:* 41-17034 to 41-17433.
*AT-6C:* 41-32073 to 41-33072, 41-33073 to 41-33819, 42-3884 to 42-4243, 42-43847 to 42-44411, 42-48772 to 42-49069.
*AT-6D:** 41-33820 to 41-34122, 41-34123 to 41-34372, 42-44412 to 42-44746, 42-84163 to 42-85912, 42-86013 to 42-86562, 44-80845 to 44-81369, 81 for Brazil.
*AT-6F:* 44-81645 to 44-81669.
*SNJ-1:* 1552 to 1567.
*SNJ-2:* 2008 to 2043, 2548 to 2572.
*SNJ-3:* 6755 to 7024, 01771 to 01976,* 05435 to 05526.*
*SNJ-4:* 05527 to 05674, 09817 to 10316, 26427 to 27851, 51350 to 51676.
*SNJ-5:* 43638 to 44037, 51677 to 52049,* 84819 to 85093, 90582 to 91101.*
*SNJ-6:* 111949 to 112359.
*Harvard IIB (AT-16):* FE267 to FE999, FH100 to FH166, FS661 to FS999, FT100 to FT460, FX198 to FX497, KF100 to KF999, 3034 to 3133 (RCAF), 3234 to 3343 (RCAF).
*Wirraway:* A20-3 to A20-757.
*T-6J:* 51-17089 to 51-17231, 52-8493 to 52-8612, 53-4615 to 53-4636.
*Sk 14:* 603-609, 672-699, 5810-5827, 14001-14060.
*Sk 14A:* 5828-5850.

\* Included in these batches are aircraft procured by USAF and transferred to US Navy; duplication of numbers causes apparent inaccuracy in overall production total.

# XB–21

Design work on the first North American bomber began at Inglewood during 1935 and the prototype emerged in March 1937 as a clean but somewhat portly mid-wing aeroplane in the same general category as the Douglas B–18, then already in production for the Air Corps. The NA–21 was an attempt to improve on the B–18's performance whilst using the same formula, and it was powered by two 1,200hp Pratt & Whitney R–2180–1 Hornet engines, with F–10 turbo-superchargers.

With a crew of six, the NA–21 was relatively heavily armed, with single 0·30in machine guns in each of five positions including a ball-type turret in the nose, a dorsal turret, two waist positions and a ventral position. A maximum bomb-load of 10,000lb could be carried over short ranges, or 2,200lb for 1,900 miles.

*North American XB–21 (NA–39).*

After some small changes, including a reduction in rudder area, the NA–21 was accepted for testing at Wright Field as the XB–21, but a planned order for five YB–21s was not confirmed and the XB–21 ended its life, with the nose and dorsal turrets removed, as a hack at Wright Field.

## Specification

| | |
|---|---|
| SPAN | 95ft |
| LENGTH | 61ft 9in |
| HEIGHT | 14ft 9in |
| WING AREA | 1,120 sq ft |
| GROSS WEIGHT | 27,253lb |
| MAX OVERLOAD WEIGHT | 40,000lb |
| MAX SPEED | 220mph |
| CRUISING SPEED | 190mph |
| RANGE | 1,960 miles |

## Production
38–485.

# NA–35

In mid-1937, North American began development of a primary trainer, intended to complement the basic and advanced trainer that had derived from the original NA–16. Of all-metal construction, this NA–35 design was typical of primary trainers of its era, with a low wing, open cockpits in tandem and a Menasco Pirate in-line engine.

Flight testing began at the end of 1939, but the NA–35 was not successful in winning the hoped-for Army Air Corps contract, and with the rapid build-up of demand for other North American military aircraft, further work on the primary trainer was stopped. The entire design rights were sold to the Vega Aircraft subsidiary of Lockheed in 1941, and the type was put into production as the Vega 35. Two variants were certificated, the Vega 35–67 with a 125hp Pirate D4 engine, and the 35–70 with a 160hp Pirate D4B, but only four examples were built by Vega before it too found its resources fully occupied with wartime production.

## Specification

| | |
|---|---|
| SPAN | 29ft 8$\frac{7}{8}$in |
| LENGTH | 25ft 6in |
| HEIGHT | 9ft 4in |
| WING AREA | 148sq ft |
| GROSS WEIGHT | 1,760lb |
| MAX SPEED | 140mph |
| CRUISING SPEED | 125mph |
| RANGE | 305 miles |

## Production
NX14299.

*The sole North American built NA–35; Lockheed built four more as Vega 35s.*

# B–25 Mitchell

Named after one of America's foremost proponents of the use of air power, General 'Billy' Mitchell, this North American twin-engined bomber was one of the outstanding aeroplanes of World War II, as well as being the first multi-engined design by the company to proceed beyond the prototype stage. Its development began in 1938 when the USAAC asked the industry for a new twin-engined attack bomber in Circular Proposal 38–385. The North American design to this proposal, evolved by a team headed by J. L. Atwood and Raymond H.

Rice, was a big advance on the earlier XB–21 prototype, and featured a nose-wheel undercarriage, shoulder mounted wing, large transparencies covering the cockpit and nose position for gunner/bomb aimer, and twin fins and rudders.

A prototype was built at Inglewood as the NA–40, powered by two 1,100hp Pratt & Whitney R–1830–S6C3–G engines and first flown by Paul Balfour in January 1939. The NA–40 had a crew of three and with a gross weight of 19,500lb could carry a bomb load of 1,200lb. A few weeks after the first flight, the NA–40 was fitted with 1,300hp Wright GR–2600–A71 Cyclone

engines, and as the NA–40–2 (sometimes NA–40B) it went to Wright Field for testing during March. Two weeks later it crashed, as a result of pilot error, and the Air Corps selected the Douglas A–20 to meet its attack bomber requirement.

Further development of the NA–40 design was requested by the Air Corps to suit it for a medium bomber rôle and many improvements were incorporated in the NA–62 design on which work proceeded during 1939. This was ordered straight into production 'off the drawing board' in September of that year, when a contract worth $11.7million was awarded, for 184

*The NA–40, progenitor of the Mitchell.*

aircraft. The first of these flew on August 19th, 1940, and the name Mitchell was adopted for it. Compared with the NA-40, the Mitchell had a widened fuselage to allow side-by-side seating for two pilots; the wing dropped to the mid position; increased weights and performance, and two 1,700hp Wright Cyclone R-2600-9 engines. The first aircraft was tested with two different fin-and-rudder shapes before the final design was evolved. A further change, made after nine aircraft had been delivered, introduced a gull wing arrangement in place of root-to-tip dihedral.

Initial aircraft off the line were designated B-25, only 24 being built before the introduction of self-sealing fuel tanks and armour protection for the pilots changed the designation of the next forty aircraft to B-25A. These were the first version of the Mitchell to become operational, aircraft of the 17th Bombardment Group (Medium) being responsible for the destruction of a Japanese submarine in the Pacific on December 24th, 1941.

Subsequent large-scale production of the Mitchell throughout the war resulted in numerous versions, the differences being mostly concerned with armament and power plant. The B-25B, of which 120 were built and 119 delivered to the USAAF (one crashing before delivery) introduced dorsal and ventral Bendix electrically-

Top right: *First production B-25 (NA-62) with constant wing dihedral from root to tip and original fin-and-rudder shape.*

Right: *B-25C Mitchell (NA-90) operating in the Middle East, 1942.*

operated turrets, the ventral unit being fully retractable and periscopically-sighted; tail guns, fitted in the earlier models, were removed. On April 18th, 1942, 16 B–25Bs manned by volunteer crews from the 17th B Group and the 89th Reconnaissance Squadron and led by Lt Col James H. Doolittle, flew off the deck of the USS *Hornet* at a distance of 800 miles from the Japanese coast to make a daring raid on Tokyo and other Japanese cities. The raid was of psychological rather than strategic importance but demonstrated the Mitchell's ability to operate successfully under arduous conditions.

The introduction of an auto-pilot, R–2600–13 engines, extra fuel capacity and bomb racks under the wings and fuselage led to a change of designation, to B–25C. Contracts for this version for use by the USAAF totalled 1,163; in addition 150 each were ordered for China and Britain with American Defense Aid funds and the Netherlands ordered 162 for use in the East Indies, but the latter aircraft had not been delivered by the time Japanese forces occupied the NEI, and they were acquired by the USAAF instead. Actual quantities delivered to foreign nations did not conform to the contracts listed; pressures of wartime events inevitably led to some shuffling. The RAF actually received 162 B–25Cs (possibly the aircraft originally

Top right: *B–25G (NA–96), the first Mitchell variant to carry the 75-lb gun in the nose.*

Right: *A US Navy PBJ–1H (NA–98) showing the forward location of the dorsal turret.*

intended for the Netherlands) and designated them Mitchell IIs, having previously accepted 23 B–25Bs as Mitchell Is. In addition to China, Russia received a quantity of B–25Cs as part of total lend-lease deliveries to the Soviet Union of 870 Mitchells. The US Navy received 50 B–25Cs from Air Force contracts and designated them PBJ–1Cs.

The rapid build-up of orders for Mitchells led North American to set up a second production line at Kansas City and this factory began production with a model equivalent to the B–25C, designated B–25D. Production totalled 2,290, of which 371 were supplied to Britain as Mitchell IIs and others were included in the total delivered to Russia. As PBJ–1Ds, the US Navy received 152 from USAAF contracts.

A major innovation made on the Mitchell in 1942 produced one of the most heavily-armed attack bombers of the war. This was the B–25G, which had a standard Army 75mm gun, firing 15lb shells, mounted in the nose, with a supply of 21 rounds. Two 0·50in Browning guns were also nose-mounted, to help to aim the cannons accurately, and four more machine guns were located in the dorsal and ventral turrets. Five Mitchells on the B–25C contract were completed as B–25Gs and 400 more were produced at Inglewood, of

Top left: *A B–25G supplied to the RAF as Mitchell II Srs II, serial FR209.*

Left: *The RAF Mitchell FR 209 modified to B–25J standard.*

*B–25J (NA–108) in RAAF service, showing package guns on front fuselage.*

which two were supplied to the RAF on lend-lease and one went to the Navy as a PBJ–1G. Further refinement of the idea produced the B–25H, with an improved version of the 75mm gun, four 0·50s in the nose, four similar guns in packs on each side of the front fuselage, two in a dorsal turret located further forward, one each side in new waist positions and two in the tail. In addition to this potent punch, the B–25H could carry up to 3,200lb of bombs or a torpedo. Of 1,000 built, 248 went to the US Navy as PBJ–1Hs. One B–25H (43–4406) was experimentally fitted with Pratt & Whitney R–2800 engines but crashed while on test.

The final production variant was the B–25J which had the same fuselage and armament as the B–25H described above, but the original bombardier-type nose containing three 0·50in guns in place of the 75mm weapon. Deliveries to the USAAF totalled 4,318; another 72 were built but scrapped at the end of the war, and 415 more on order were cancelled. The US Navy received 255 as PBJ–1J and the RAF received 314 as Mitchell III; 29 went to Brazil on lend-lease, and others to Russia. The Mitchell also saw operational service with the Dutch Air Force, a total of 249 of various sub-types being supplied under lend-lease for use by the Royal Netherlands

Indies Army Air Division operating in the Pacific area. B–25s continued in service with USAF units until 1960, and elsewhere for several more years. The RCAF acquired 75 B–25Js from the USAAF in 1951 to supplement seventy ex–RAF Mitchell IIIs and these served until 1963. A few were still serving in Brazil and Venezuela in 1971.

In addition to the main production versions described above, the following variants were designated:

*XB–25E:* One B–25C airframe (42–32281) with hot-air leading-edge de-icing.
*XB–25F:* As above with electric de-icing.

*A B–25C (NA–93) in the markings of the Chinese Nationalist Air Force.*

39

*CB–25J:* Post-war conversions for utility rôle.

*VB–25J:* Post-war conversions for staff transport.

*AT–24A:* B–25D stripped for use as advanced trainer.

*AT–24B:* B–25G as above.

*AT–24C:* B–25C as above.

*AT–24D:* B–25J as above; total of 60 AT–24 conversions in the four variants.

*TB–25C:* AT–24C redesignated in 1947.

*TB–25D:* AT–24A redesignated in 1947.

*TB–25G:* AT–24B redesignated in 1947.

*TB–25J:* AT–24D redesignated in 1947, plus more B–25J conversions post-war to total over 600.

*TB–25K:* 117 B–25J modified as E–1 fire control trainers, by Hughes, in 1951.

*TB–25L:* 90 B–25J modified as pilot trainers, by Hayes, in 1951.

*TB–25M:* 40 B–25J modified as E–5 fire control radar trainers, by Hughes in 1952.

*TB–25N:* 47 B–25J modified as pilot

Top left: *An RCAF Mitchell II modified to the standard of the USAF's F–10 reconnaissance version with nose cameras.*

Left: *A post-war Mitchell modification for transport use, as CB–25J.*

Top right: *With a lengthened nose and internal changes, this Mitchell trainer prototype was a North American demonstrator, with civil registration N5126N.*

Right: *The last Mitchell variant designated was the TB–25N, originally a pilot trainer but shown in service here in 1956 as a target tug.*

trainers, with R–2600–29A engines, by Hayes, in 1954.

*F–10:* 10 B–25D modified by NA in 1943 for photo-reconnaissance training, with R–260–29 engines.

## Specification

| | |
|---|---|
| SPAN | 67ft 7in |
| LENGTH | 52ft 11in (B–25C) |
| | 51ft (B–25H) |
| HEIGHT | 15ft 10in |
| WING AREA | 610sq ft |
| GROSS WEIGHT | 34,000lb (B–25C) |
| | 36,047lb (B–25H) |
| MAX SPEED | 284mph at 15,000ft (B–25C) |
| | 275mph at 13,000ft (B–25H) |
| CRUISING SPEED | 233mph (B–25C) |
| | 230mph (B–25H) |
| RANGE | 1,500 miles (B–25C) |
| | 1,350 miles (B–25H) |

## Production

*NA–40/NA–40–2:* X14221.
*B–25:* 40–2165 to 40–2188.
*B–25A:* 40–2189 to 40–2228.
*B–25B:* 40–2229 to 40–2348.
*B–25C:* 41–12434 to 41–13296, 42–32233 to 42–32532, 42–53332 to 42–53493, (ordered by Netherlands as N5–122 to N5–283), 42–64502 to 42–64801.
*B–25D:* 41–29648 to 41–30847, 42–87113 to 42–87612, 43–3280 to 43–3869.
*B–25G:* 42–32384 to 42–32388, 42–64802 to 42–65201.
*B–25H:* 43–4105 to 43–5104.
*B–25J:* 43–3870 to 43–4104, 43–27473 to 43–28222, 43–35946 to 43–36245, 44–28711 to 44–31510, 44–86692 to 44–86897, 45–8801 to 45–8899.

# NA-44

Among the alternative rôles proposed for derivatives of the basic NA-16 design was that of light bomber or attack aircraft. Armed versions of the aircraft had already been evolved in 1936 when the NA-26 was produced as a demonstrator in the USAAC Basic Combat Trainer competition.

In order to satisfy this requirement and the interest of other potential customers, a new demonstrator was built as the NA-44, flying for the first time in 1938. This incorporated features introduced in the production derivatives of the NA-26 (the BC-1 series) plus an all-metal fuselage, integral fuel tanks in the wings and a Wright R-1820-F52 Cyclone engine. Successful demonstrations led to orders for the basic

NA-44 version being placed in November 1939, by Siam (for 10 NA-69s) and in 1940 by Brazil (for 30 NA-72s) and Chile (for 12 NA-74s).

These attack bomber versions carried five 0·30in machine guns, two in the cowling, two in the wings and one on a flexible mount in the rear cockpit. Up to 400lb of bombs could be carried beneath the wings. Deliveries to Brazil began in

*The NA-44 light attack bomber demonstrator in original markings as NX-18981.*

July 1940, followed by the aircraft for Chile. Those for Siam, however, were en route at the time of the Japanese attack on that country and were requisitioned by the USAAC in the Philippines, where they were intercepted on board ship. Given the designation A–27, these ten aircraft were pressed into service with General Mac-Arthur's forces in the Pacific.

The original NA–44 demonstrator ended up in Canada, being taken on strength by the RCAF on August 23rd, 1940 as serial 3344, and remaining on strength until February 1947.

## Specification (NA–44)

| | |
|---|---|
| SPAN | 42ft |
| LENGTH | 29ft |
| HEIGHT | 12ft 2in |
| WING AREA | 258sq ft |
| GROSS WEIGHT | 6,700lb |
| MAX SPEED | 250mph at 11,500ft |
| CRUISING SPEED | 220mph |
| RANGE | 575 miles with 400lb bombs |

## Production

*NA–44:* NX18981.
*NA–69 (A–27):* 41–18890/18899.
*NA–72:* 30 for Brazil.
*NA–74:* 12 for Chile.

*Top right: The NA–44 photographed at Trenton in 1946 after service with the RCAF throughout the war.*

*Right: One of the NA–69s intended for Siam, photographed after being taken over by the USAAC in the Philippines, with the designation A–27.*

# NA–50, NA–68

With the trainer derivatives of the NA–16 firmly established in production by 1938, North American investigated a number of ways in which the versatility of the basic design could be extended. This line of development resulted in a single-seat fighter, with a shorter wing and more powerful engine, but recognisably a relative of the AT–6 Harvard in appearance.

As the NA–50, seven examples of this fighter were ordered by Peru, delivery being completed in May 1939. The engine was an 870hp Wright R–1820–77 Cyclone driving a three-blade constant speed propeller, and the armament comprised two 0·30in Colt machine guns in the cowling and provision for 550lb of bombs. Fuselage construction was of metal, and the 170-US gal of fuel was carried in integral tanks. Ring and bead sights were fitted ahead of the cockpit. The NA–50s saw brief operational service in 1941 when Peruvian forces were in action against those of Ecuador.

Six NA–68s ordered by the Royal Thai Air Force in 1940 were basically the same

Top left: *NA–50 single-seat fighter awaiting delivery to Peru.*

Left: *The NA–68 fighter, derived from the NA–50, in civil markings for testing in the USA.*

Right: *An NA–68 armed and camouflaged in preparation for delivery to Thailand.*

as the Peruvian aircraft. Principal differences were the use of the more angular rudder by that time introduced on later AT-6s; a modified landing gear and the addition of two 22mm cannon in fairings under the wings. Completed in November 1940, the NA-68s were requisitioned by the US government shortly before delivery, because of Japan's aggressive moves against Thailand and the likelihood that the NA-68s would therefore fall into Japanese hands.

The NA-68s were then assigned to USAAF advanced fighter training schools, retaining their original Thai camouflage with American stars over the roundels. Although intended only as trainers, and used with the cannon removed from the wings, these aircraft were designated P-64 in the pursuit series because they were single-seaters. One survived the war and found its way to Mexico where it was used (as XB-KUU) for a time before returning to the US. This aircraft was fitted with an R-1820-66 and had a modified cowling, with guns removed.

## Specification (NA-68)

| | |
|---|---|
| SPAN | 37ft 3in |
| LENGTH | 27ft |
| HEIGHT | 19ft |
| WING AREA | 227·5sq ft |
| GROSS WEIGHT | 6,800lb |
| MAX SPEED | 270mph at 8,700ft |
| CRUISING SPEED | 235mph |
| RANGE | 630 miles |

## Production

*NA-50:* Seven aircraft.
*P-64:* 41-19082/19087.

# XB–28

Work on a twin-engined high altitude bomber based on the B–25 Mitchell began in 1939 at about the same time that the Mitchell itself was being finalised in the light of flight testing of the NA–40 prototypes. Thus, while the production form of the NA–40 was identified as the NA–62, the high altitude variant was the NA–63. The principal difference, as originally planned, was that the NA–63 had a circular-section fuselage containing a pressurised cabin accommodating the crew of five. A

*The first prototype of the XB–28 (NA–63).*

contract for three prototypes was placed on February 13th, 1940.

By the time the first of these, designated XB–28, was ready to fly in April 1942, many changes had been made, so that little resemblance to the Mitchell remained. The XB–28 had a single fin and rudder, and remotely controlled defensive armament in dorsal and ventral turrets and a tail barbette, each containing two 0·50in machine guns. Sighting was by means of a periscope behind the flight deck, as all three gun positions were outside the pressurised area. Three more 0·30in guns

fired forwards. The engines were 2,000hp Pratt & Whitney R–2800–11 radials. The bomb-bay could carry up to 4,000lb; and an alternative camera installation was fitted in the third prototype, which was designated XB–28A with R–2800–27 engines. This prototype crashed into the Pacific during a test flight. The second XB–28 was cancelled.

Pressurisation of the cabin was achieved by means of a mechanical engine-driven supercharger that maintained an equivalent pressure height of 8,000ft at altitudes of up to 33,000ft. Sealing of the cabin was by means of rubber strips sandwiched between all riveted joints, and a plastic compound was sprayed over the entire internal skin. Cabin heaters were incorporated in the ducts that supplied pressurised air to the cabin.

The XB–28 performed well and demonstrated an excellent high altitude capability, but a requirement for such a type of twin-engined bomber was not established and no production took place.

## Specification (XB–28)

| | |
|---|---|
| SPAN | 72ft 7in |
| LENGTH | 56ft 5in |
| HEIGHT | 14ft |
| WING AREA | 676sq ft |
| GROSS WEIGHT | 37,200lb |
| MAX SPEED | 372mph at 25,000ft |
| CRUISING SPEED | 255mph |
| RANGE | 2,040 miles with 600lb bomb load |

## Production
*XB–28: 40-3056.*
*XB–28A: 40-3058.*

# P-51 Mustang, Cavalier, Enforcer

One of the few truly great aeroplanes of World War II, the North American Mustang owed its inception to British rather than American requirements, and achieved its greatest success when fitted with a British engine. The product of a still-young design team, headed by Raymond H. Rice and Edgar Schmued, with unfettered ideas about the design of a combat aeroplane, the Mustang was also notable for the speed with which it was designed, built and put into operation. By the time the war ended in 1945 (bringing cancellation of contracts then in hand for 5,973 Mustangs) 15,586 aircraft of this type had been built in North American's factory—yet design work did not begin until 1940.

In the early months of that year, the British Air Purchasing Commission was seeking to purchase large quantities of aircraft in America to strengthen the hard-pressed RAF. None of the fighters then available from US manufacturers was considered to be ideal for European combat conditions—although many stop-gap orders were placed—and the possibility of having an entirely new type developed specifically for the RAF was discussed with J. H. Kindelberger, NAA's president, in April 1940. With enthusiastic support from the

Top left: *The NA-73X, prototype of the Mustang family.*

Left: *The first Mustang (NA-73) built on British contract, AG345.*

47

company and an approving nod from the US government, which stipulated that two early production models should be made available for USAAC testing at no cost, the project got under way in April 1940 with a 120-day target for completion of the prototype.

The prototype was identified as the NA–73X and it was designed around a 1,100hp Allison V–1710–39 engine. Noticeable features of the design were its angular lines, chosen for ease of production, location of the radiator 'bath' well aft below the cockpit to preserve clean lines for the front fuselage, and a laminar-flow wing section for low drag at high speed. Provision was made for four wing guns and two in the lower nose cowling. First flown by Vance Breeze on October 26th, 1940, the NA–73X carried civil registration NX19998 as a company-financed prototype. It eventually crashed and was destroyed, but not before it had demonstrated excellent low-level performance and outstanding handling characteristics.

The British Air Purchasing Commission was well satisfied with the NA–73X and confirmed an order for 320 NA–73s, for which the name Apache was briefly considered before Mustang was adopted. A second order for 300 followed soon after,

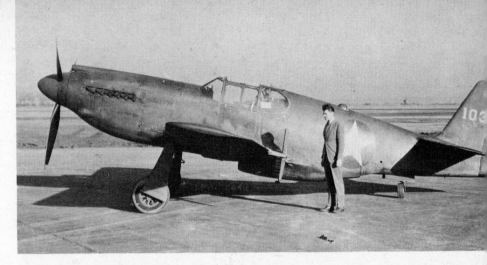

Top right: *The tenth production Mustang airframe, completed as an XP–51 (NA–73) and shown here while on test by NACA at Langley Field.*

Right: *An experimental installation of 40mm Vickers 'S' cannon on Mustang I (NA–83) AM106.*

these being built as NA–82s, but all were Mustang Is in RAF service, having an armament of four 0·50in and four 0·30in machine guns—two of the former in the nose below the engine and the remainder in the wings. The Allison F3R engine was rated only for low altitudes and the Mustang Is were therefore assigned to tactical reconnaissance duties, carrying an oblique camera in the cockpit behind the pilot. The first production aircraft flew at Inglewood on May 1st, 1941 and the type entered service with No 2 Squadron, RAF, in July 1942.

Fulfilling its obligation to the USAAF, North American built two additional NA–73s (actually the 4th and 10th production aircraft) which went to Wright Field as XP–51s. Successful trials, and the high speed of 382mph then demonstrated, led the USAAF to include the Mustang in its procurement plans—still primarily in a low-altitude tactical rôle. Orders were placed for 310 P–51As, with armament of four 0·50in wing guns and the 1,200hp Allison V–1710–81 engine, and 500 A–36As, which had six 0·50in guns including two in the nose, wing racks for two 500lb bombs, dive brakes and the 1,325hp V–1710–87 engine. The latter were the first USAAF Mustangs to go into operation, in Sicily and Italy during 1943.

Using Defence Aid Funds, the USAAF also ordered 150 P–51s for supply to the RAF as Mustang IAs. These had a wing armament of four 20mm cannon but were

*A Mustang I (NA–83) AM190 retained in North America and used for the prototype installation of four 20mm wing guns.*

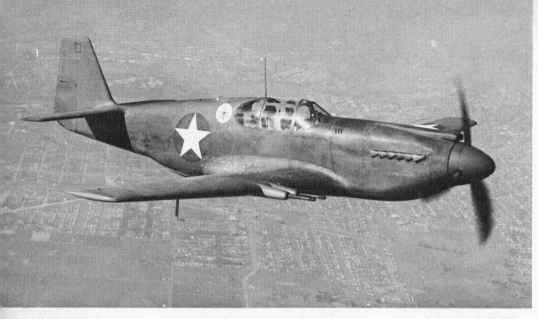

otherwise similar to the Mustang Is. Of this total 57 were retained for service with the USAAF, but under subsequent lend-lease arrangements, fifty of the P–51As referred to above were supplied to Britain as Mustang IIs, plus a single example of the A–36A for evaluation.

The idea of installing the Rolls-Royce Merlin in the Mustang, to improve its performance at higher altitudes, was conceived in the Spring of 1942 after one of the early Mustang Is had been flown at the AFDU by a R–R test pilot. Theoretical calculation showed that a Mustang with Merlin XX engine would achieve 393mph at 18,600ft while use of the Merlin 61 would bestow a speed of 432mph at 25,500ft. A programme to convert several Mustang Is was put in hand at the R–R test establishment at Hucknall, and the USAAF instructed North American to proceed with a similar programme to fit the 1,380hp Packard-built V–1650–3 version of the Merlin.

The first flight with a Merlin-Mustang was made at Hucknall on October 13th, 1942, the aircraft being Mustang I AL975/G and the engine being a Merlin 65. Four more aircraft were converted by Rolls-Royce, and Merlin 70 and 71 versions were

Top left: *Cannon-armed P–51 (NA–91) in North American test markings, 1942.*

Left: *USAAF P–51–1 (NA–91) reconnaissance version in experimental black and white splinter finish; oblique camera is mounted in blister at rear of cockpit.*

Right: *P–51A (NA–99) Mustangs of the USAAF with smoke curtain installation beneath the wings.*

also flown. All five aircraft were officially designated Mustang X when fitted with Merlin engine, and were distinguished by the air intake for the intercooler radiator located immediately behind the spinner. Speeds as high as 433mph were achieved, vindicating the original estimates, and conversion of 500 Mustang Is to Mustang X standard was projected. However, the latter step became unnecessary because the success of the parallel North American programme led to a switch to the Merlin engine for all subsequent Mustang production.

The two NAA prototypes were initially designated XP-78s but were completed as XP-51Bs, being converted P-51 airframes. They had a small air intake behind the spinner, strengthened airframe and wing pylons for up to 1,000lb each side. A maximum speed of 441mph was demonstrated. Production had already been put in hand at Inglewood, which built 1,988 P-51Bs with armament of four 0·50in wing guns; a second production line established by NAA at Dallas produced 1,750 of the similar P-51C. Included in these totals were 910 to be supplied to the RAF as Mustang IIIs—274 from Inglewood and 636 from Dallas.

A major improvement in all-round visibility was achieved in the next production variant, the P-51D, which had a cut-

Top right: *An A-36 (NA-97) supplied to the RAF for evaluation, showing the bomb racks and dive brakes on the wings.*

Right: *Experimental installation of a Merlin 65 by Rolls-Royce in Mustang X AM208.*

down rear fuselage and a 'tear-drop' canopy. Also standardised in this model were features that had been introduced progressively on later P–51Bs and P–51Cs, such as a six-gun wing armament, 1,695hp V–1650–7 engine and a small dorsal fin. Inglewood built 6,502 P–51Ds and Dallas built 1,454, with 271 of this total assigned to the RAF as Mustang IVs. The Dallas plant also built 1,337 P–51Ks, which differed from the 'D' only in having an Aeroproducts propeller; the RAF received 594 of these, also as Mustang IVs.

The final production version, and the fastest of all the Mustangs, was the P–51H. This was evolved through a series of experimental lightweight versions and was more than 1,000lb lighter than the P–51D, despite having increased fuel and the 2,218hp V–1650–9 engine driving a four-blade Aeroproducts propeller. A taller fin and shorter canopy were fitted, and the top speed was 487mph. Production totalled 555, with another 1,845 cancelled, together with 1,700 similar P–51Ls to have been built at Dallas. One example was supplied to the RAF.

In addition to the production models of the Mustang described above, the following versions were also designated:

*TP–51D:* Originally, ten P–51Ds were converted to two seaters by NAA with this

Top left: *First American installation of a Packard-Merlin in a Mustang IA airframe as XP–51B (NA–101).*

Left: *P–51B (NA–104) of USAAF's Eighth Air Force serving in Europe.*

53

*An RAF Mustang III with Malcolm bubble cockpit canopy and experimental rocket installation.*

designation, having full dual control in a second cockpit behind and higher than the regular pilot's position. Some P–51B and C models were converted to two-seaters at field bases and, post-war, more conversions to similar TP–51D standard were made by Temco and Cavalier.

*XP–51F:* Three lightweight prototypes with bubble canopies and V–1650–3 engines; one to the RAF.

*XP–51G:* Two prototypes, similar to XP–51F with Merlin RM–145M engines; one to the RAF.

*XP–51J:* Two prototypes similar to XP–51F with Allison V–1710–119 engines.

*P–51M:* The last production P–51D from Dallas was fitted with a V–1650–9A engine and redesignated.

*P–51–1:* See F–6 below.

*F–6:* An armed tactical reconnaissance version of the Mustang for the USAAF. The first batch of aircraft were the 57 P–51s retained from the British Defence Aid contract. They had four-cannon armament and two K–24 cameras in the fuselage. Tentatively designated F–6As, they were finally called P–51–1s.

*F–6B:* Thirty-five P–51As converted as above, with machine gun armament.

*F–6C:* Ninety-one P–51B/C conversions

with two K–24 or one K–17 plus one K–22 camera installation.

*F–6D:* Camera-equipped conversion of P–51D; 136 produced.

*F–6K:* Camera-equipped conversion of P–51K; 163 produced.

*F–51D:* Surviving P–51Ds redesignated in 1951.

*F–51K:* Surviving P–51Ks redesignated in 1951.

*RF–51D:* Surviving F–6Ds redesignated in 1951.

*RF–51K:* Surviving F–6Ks redesignated in 1951.

*TRF–51D:* Two-seat variant of RF–51D.

To meet an urgent need for a new fighter to serve with the RAAF, the Australian government acquired a license to build the Mustang in its P–51D version in 1943. One hundred sets of components were purchased from North American (included in the Inglewood production total quoted above and built as NA–110) plus one pattern aircraft tested in Australia as A68–1001. Production of the Mustang was entrusted to Commonwealth Aircraft Corporation, which used the NAA components to assemble 80 CA–17 Mustang XXs with V–1650–3 engines. The first of these flew on April 29th, 1945. Production continued with the CA–18 variant powered by the V–1650–7 engine, CAC delivering

*Top right: An early production P–51D (NA–106) with tear-drop canopy and no dorsal fin.*

*Right: Late-production P–51D (NA–109) with dorsal fin and drop tanks.*

40 as Mustang 21, 14 as Mustang 22 with oblique F24 camera in the fuselage and finally 66 Mustang 23 with Merlin 66 or 70 engines from the UK. Fourteen Mk 21s were later converted to Mk 22s. Production of 50 more CA–18s and 250 CA–21 Mustangs was cancelled, and the RAAF acquired instead 214 P–51Ds and 84 P–51Ks from the USAAF. Too late to serve in the War, the RAAF Mustangs were assigned to occupation duties in Japan and one squadron, No 77, was operational in the Korean War until April 1951, when some of these Mustangs were transferred to the Korean Air Force.

No other original production of the Mustang was undertaken, but both during and following World War II the type saw widespread service. Fifty P–51Ds were supplied to China before the war ended and forty were accepted by the RAAF for use by the Netherlands East Indies Air Force (serialled N3–601 to N3–640), while ten Mustang Is are reported to have been shipped to Russia from Britain. Post-war, major users of surplus USAAF Mustangs included the Swedish Air Force, which bought 140 in 1945/46, the Swiss Air Force, which acquired about 140, and the RCAF, which obtained thirty in 1947 and 100 more in 1950/51. Another Commonwealth Air Force, that of New Zealand, used thirty Mustangs and for its contribution to

Top left: *The XP–51G lightweight prototype with Merlin RM–14SM.*

Left: *The XP–51J lightweight model with Allison V–1710–119 engine.*

United Nations forces in Korea, the South African Air Force bought 95 P–51Ds in 1950/51—losing a total of 73 of these in the course of the conflict.

Under the terms of the Rio Pact of Mutual Defence signed in 1947, the USA supplied surplus Mustangs to several South American nations, including Bolivia, Brazil, Cuba, Guatemala, Haiti, Honduras, Nicaragua and Uruguay. Italy acquired about fifty from USAAF sources soon after the end of the war, and Indonesia inherited some of the P–51Ds and P–51Ks operated by the NEI Air Force when the country became independent. Disposal of the Mustangs operated by the Swedish Air Force allowed Dominica to acquire 32 in 1952 and Israel obtained 25 from the same source. Other user nations included Somalia and the Philippines.

A number of 'civilianised' Mustangs appeared in US air races immediately following World War II and these sported a variety of modifications designed to enhance their performance. Continuing interest in the aircraft among civil pilots led in the mid 'fifties to the marketing of a two-seat executive Mustang by Trans-Florida Aviation Inc. This model was named Cavalier 2000 and subsequently the name of the company marketing it was changed to Cavalier Aircraft Corp. Basically an F–51D, the Cavalier 2000 had new

*Top right: A tall-finned P–51H (NA–126).*

*Right: A P–51K (NA–111) over the Great Sind Desert near Karachi.*

instrumentation and avionics, a passenger seat in tandem behind the pilot, a modified bubble canopy and 110-US gal wing-tip tanks stressed for aerobatics. With a maximum permissible speed of 505mph at sea level, the Cavalier 2000 was marketed at $32,500 in 1961.

Further variants of the type were evolved subsequently, as follows:

*Cavalier 750:* No tip tanks.
*Cavalier 1200:* As 750 with two additional 48-US gal internal wing tanks.
*Cavalier 1500:* As 750 with two additional 63-US gal internal wing tanks.
*Cavalier 2500:* As 2000 with two additional 60-US gal internal wing tanks.

In addition to the executive Mustang, Cavalier Aircraft received a contract from the USAF in 1967 to supply a small batch of remanufactured F-51Ds for MAP delivery to South American nations. These aircraft had V-1650-7 engines, the taller P-51H-type fins, strengthened wings with six 0-50in guns and eight hardpoints. All

Top left: *An F-6D conversion of a P-51D, with camera port in rear fuselage.*

Left: *Two-seat TP-51D conversion of the Mustang by Temco.*

Top right: *A Mustang in use as a test-bed for ram-jet engines at the wing tips.*

Right: *The Mustang 'Beguine' used by Bill Odom in the 1949 Thompson Trophy Race, with the ventral radiator replaced by wing tip radiators, reduced wing span, a boosted Merlin engine and other modifications.*

had a second seat behind the pilot, and one was a TF–51D with full dual control. In 1968, the US Army purchased two Cavalier conversions for use as chase aircraft; these two-seaters were unarmed and had wing-tip tanks.

As a private venture, Cavalier developed two counter-insurgency patrol and attack aircraft from the F–51D. The first, known as the Cavalier Mustang II had a 1,760hp Rolls–Royce Merlin 620 engine and strengthened airframe to carry a wide variety of weapons beneath the wings. Fixed wing-tip tanks of 110–US gal capacity each were fitted, giving an unrefuelled duration of $7\frac{1}{2}$ hours. The Mustang II first flew in December 1967.

Flown in late 1968, the Turbo Mustang III had an airframe similar to that of the Mustang II, but was powered by a 1,740hp Rolls-Royce Dart 510 turboprop and additional structural and aerodynamic modification to permit higher speeds to be achieved. Based on flight testing of this aircraft, Cavalier put in hand two additional prototypes—one a single-seater and the other a two-seater—to be powered by the 2,535hp Lycoming T55–L–9 turboprop. Before completion, these aircraft were taken over by Piper for development with the name Enforcer. The first prototype flew on April 29th, 1971 but crashed on July 12th. The second prototype was completed and was one of three types chosen for evaluation in the USAF Pave Coin project in 1971, intended to select an 'off-the-shelf' specialised tactical aircraft for Forward Air Control and light strike missions. The inclusion in this evaluation of an aircraft the basic design of which was more than thirty years old was clearly a

great tribute to the soundness of North American's work on the original NA–73X.

## Specification

| | |
|---|---|
| SPAN | 37ft (No tip tanks) |
| | 40ft 1in (Cavalier 2000) |
| LENGTH | 32ft 3in (P–51B) |
| | 33ft 4in (P–51H) |
| HEIGHT | 12ft 2in (P–51B) |
| | 13ft 8in (P–51H) |
| WING AREA | 233sq ft (No tip tanks) |
| | 272sq ft (Cavalier 2000) |
| GROSS WEIGHT | 11,800lb (P–51B) |
| | 11,054lb (P–51H) |
| | 10,500lb (Cavalier 2000) |
| | 14,000lb (Turbo Mustang III) |
| MAX SPEED | 440mph (P–51B) |
| | 487mph (P–51H) |
| | 457mph (Cavalier 2000) |
| CRUISING SPEED | 362mph (P–51B) |
| | 380mph (P–51H) |
| | 370mph (Cavalier 2000) |
| | 380mph (Turbo Mustang III) |
| RANGE | 400 miles (P–51B) |
| | 850 miles (P–51H) |
| | 2,000 miles (Cavalier 2,000) |
| | 2,300 miles (Turbo Mustang III) |

Top left: *Cavalier 2000 two-seat conversion of the Mustang for private use.*

Left: *A two-seat Cavalier-built F–51D built for the USAF in 1967.*

Right: *The Cavalier Mustang II prototype.*

## Production

*NA–73X:* NX19998

*Mustang I:* AG345 to AG664, AL958 to AL999, AM100 to AM257, AP164 to AP263.

*XP–51:* 41–038 to 41–039.

*P–51/Mustang IA:* 41–37320 to 41–37469, (FD418 to FD567).

*A–36A:* 42–83663 to 42–84162.

*P–51A:* 43–6003 to 43–6312.

*XP–51B:* (41–37352 and 41–37421).

*P–51B:* 42–106429 to 42–106538, 42–106541 to 42–106978, 43–6313 to 42–7202, 43–12093 to 42–12492, 43–24752 to 43–24901.

*P–51C:* 42–102979 to 42–103978, 43–24902 to 43–25251, 44–10753 to 44–11152.

*P51D–NA:* 42–106539 to 42–106540, 44–13253 to 44–15752, 44–63160 to 44–64159, 44–72027 to 44–75026.

*P51D–NT:* 44–11153 to 44–11352, 44–12853 to 44–13252, 44–84390 to 44–84989, 45–11343 to 45–11742.

*XP–51F:* 43–43332 to 43–43334.

*XP–51G:* 43–43335 to 43–43336.

*P–51H:* 44–64160 to 44–64714.

*XP–51J:* 44–76027 to 44–76028.

*P–51K:* 44–11353 to 44–12852.

*P–51M:* 45–11743.

*CA–17 Mustang XX:* A68–1 to A68–80.

*CA–18 Mustang 21:* A68–81 to A68–120.

*CA–18 Mustang 22:* A68–187 to A68–200.

*CA–18 Mustang 23:* A68–121 to A68–186.

Top right: *With a Dart turboprop engine, the Cavalier Turbo Mustang III.*

Right: *Still basically a Mustang—the heavily armed, turboprop-engined Piper Enforcer of 1971.*

# F–82 Twin Mustang

One of the most unusual products of the North American company to reach production, the Twin Mustang was a highly ingenious solution to the problem of providing a very long range escort fighter at short notice. Operations by the USAAF in the Pacific area during 1943 showed that the pilots of single-seat fighters were being subjected to very severe strains by the lengths of typical missions. To provide a two-seat fighter whilst retaining the desirable features of the P–51 Mustang and also minimising development time, North American adopted the simple expedient of joining two Mustang fuselages and outer wing panels together by a new centre section and tailplane.

The first of two NA–120 prototypes designated XP–82 flew on April 15th, 1945, some sixteen months after the start of work on the project. These aircraft had two Packard V–1650–23/25 Merlin engines with opposite rotation to eliminate engine torque while a third prototype, the XP–82A, had Allison V–1710–119 engines both rotating in the same direction. Before the first flight, the USAAF ordered 500 P–82Bs with Merlin engines but only twenty of these were built before the whole-sale cancellation of production contracts after VJ-Day. Of these, two were later converted to night fighters, carrying radar in a large pod beneath the centre section and with one cockpit equipped for a radar operator instead of pilot. These two aircraft had two different types of radar— SCR 720 in the P–82C and APS–4 in the P–82D.

To replace the Northrop P–61 Black

*The second prototype XP–82 (NA–120) Twin Mustang.*

63

Widow, the USAF ordered 100 P–82Fs with SCR 720 and fifty P–82Gs with APS–4 in 1946, together with 100 P–82Es without radar for service in the escort fighter rôle. They went into service with Air Defense Command during 1947 and were available for deployment in support of United Nations forces in Korea. An F–82G flying with the 68th Fighter (All-Weather) Squadron of the 8th F–B Wing is credited with the first air-to-air victory of that war in a combat which was also the first in which a pilot serving with the USAF (rather than the USAAF) scored a 'kill'. By this time the Twin Mustangs had taken the F–82 designation in place of P–82.

North American completed fourteen of the night fighters as F–82Hs for service in Alaska, with special features to permit cold-weather operations, this action reducing the F–82F contract to 91 and the F–82G deliveries to 45. The Twin Mustang was the last piston-engined fighter ordered in quantity by the USAF.

**Specification (F–82E)**

| | |
|---|---|
| SPAN | 51ft 3in |
| LENGTH | 39ft 1in |
| HEIGHT | 13ft 10in |
| WING AREA | 408sq ft |
| GROSS WEIGHT | 24,864lb |
| MAX SPEED | 465mph at 21,000ft |
| CRUISING SPEED | 304mph |
| RANGE | 2,500 miles |

**Production**

*XP–82:* 44–83886 to 44–83887.
*XP–82A:* 44–83888.
*P–82B:* 44–65160 to 44–65179.
*P–82C:* 44–65169.
*P–82D:* 44–65170.
*P–82E:* 46–255 to 46–354.
*P–82F:* 46–405 to 46–504.
*P–82G:* 46–355 to 46–404.
*F–82H:* 46–384 to 46–388, 46–496 to 46–504.

# Production of Other Types

In addition to the design and construction of aircraft of its own design, the North American company has undertaken the production of certain other types. Primarily, this occurred during World War II, although one of the company's very earliest contracts involved the production of 161 sets of floats (one main and two wing-tip) for Curtiss SOC–1 floatplane for the US Navy. These were built at the

*The P–82C (NA–123) night fighter with radome under the centre section.*

original Dundalk, Maryland, plant under the NA–17 designation but a second batch of 48 sets for SOC–2s were built (as NA–24) at Inglewood.

Making a significant contribution to US four-engined bomber production, despite the large quantities of P–51s and B–25s it was also turning out, North American established a Consolidated Liberator assembly line at the Dallas plant in 1942, and began deliveries in 1943. Two versions were built, both under the designation NA–95, production comprising 430 B–24Gs —a version similar to the Consolidated-built B–24D—and 536 B–24Js. Another 734 B–24s on order from North American were cancelled at the end of the war, together with a plan to build 1,000 Lockheed Shooting Stars as P–80Ns (NA–137) at Kansas.

Also at Dallas, a production line was set up in 1945 for Fairchild Packet transports, and North American received a contract to build 792 of a version designated C–82N (NA–135). Only three of these were completed before VJ-Day cancellation of the programme. Plans for North American to participate in B–29 production were abandoned.

### Production
B–24G: 42–78045 to 42–78474.
B–24J: 42–78475 to 42–78794, 44–28061 to 44–28276.
C–82N: 45–25436 to 45–25438.

*North American B–45A (NA–147), the USAF's first jet bomber.*

# B–45 Tornado

America's first four-jet bomber to fly, and to enter service, was born on the drawing boards of the North American company during 1944/45. With the war in Europe nearing its end but the results of German research into swept-back wings not yet available to American designers, the NA–130 was laid out along conventional lines, its only really radical feature being the use of four General Electric J35–A–4 jet engines, paired in nacelles one under each wing. Like the Mitchell, the new North American aircraft had a shoulder wing, two pilots, a bombardier in the nose and a gunner in the tail, without pressurisation.

Three prototypes were ordered as XB–45s in 1945 and the first of these flew at Edwards Air Force Base on March 17th, 1947. The USAF bought a production batch of 96 (plus one 'flying static' test vehicle) with deliveries starting in 1948, the first aircraft going to the 47th Bombardment Group at Barksdale AFB, which then became the USAF's first jet-equipped bomber unit. The first 22 B–45As were delivered with J35–A–11 engines but the J47–GE–9 was then adopted as the standard power plant.

The B–45B, with changed radar and fire control equipment, being cancelled before production, the next variant of the Tornado to appear was the B–45C. Only ten were built, differing from the B–45A in having uprated, water-injection J47–GE–13/15 engines, single point refuelling, higher gross weight, strengthened airframe and wing-tip fuel tanks containing 1,200 US gal of fuel each. These same new features were incorporated in the 33 RB–45Cs that were delivered between June 1950 and October 1951, but these aircraft also had twelve cameras mounted in four groups in the nose and centre fuselage. Contracts for

another two B–45C and 49 RB–45C were cancelled.

Because of their high performance, B–45s were adopted for various research rôles, and several became flying test beds for new jet engines mounted in pods under the bomb-bay, or in retractable installations in the fuselage. Allison, General Electric, Pratt & Whitney and Westinghouse engines of various types were tested in this way, the aircraft in some cases being designated JB–45A or JB–45C. Other Tornadoes were adapted as drone and missile directors designated DB–45A and DB–45C, and 14 B–45As were converted for use as target tugs, with reel and cable assemblies in the bomb–bays, being then redesignated TB–45As.

## Specification (RB–45C)

| | |
|---|---|
| SPAN | 96ft (over tip tanks) |
| LENGTH | 75ft 11in |
| HEIGHT | 25ft 2in |
| WING AREA | 1,175sq ft |
| GROSS WEIGHT | 110,721lb |
| MAX SPEED | 570mph at 4,000ft |
| COMBAT SPEED | 506mph |
| RANGE | 2,530 miles |

## Production

*XB–45:* 45–59479 to 45–59481.
*B–45A:* 47–001 to 47–097.
*B–45C:* 48–001 to 48–010.
*RB–45C:* 48–011 to 48–043.

Top right: *RB–45C (NA–153) reconnaissance bomber.*

Right: *An RB–45C used as a jet engine test bed.*

66

# FJ-1 Fury

Although it cannot be rated an outstanding success operationally, the FJ-1 Fury is significant in North American history as the company's first jet fighter design. It originated, as the NA-134, during 1944 to meet US Navy requirements for a high-performance carrier-borne fighter on which to obtain added experience of the then-new method of propulsion. The project was based on a wing design closely resembling that of the Mustang—the excellent characteristics of which had been clearly established—but the fuselage was completely new and in order to achieve a straight-through flow of air for the centrally-mounted General Electric J-35 engine the cockpit was located above the intake duct. This produced a short, squat fuselage, with internal tankage supplemented by fixed wing-tip tanks.

The Navy ordered three prototypes of the NA-134 on January 1st, 1945, and on May 28th the same year followed up with a contract for 100 NA-141 production models. Prototypes and production aircraft were designated XFJ-1 and FJ-1 respectively and the name Fury was adopted. First flight of the XFJ-1, with a 3,820lb st J35-GE-2 engine, was made on November 27th, 1946, at Los Angeles, where production took place.

With an armament of six 0·50in machine guns in the fuselage nose around the intake, and powered by Allison-built 4,000lb st J35-A-2 or -4 engines, the FJ-1s started to reach the Navy in March 1948 and were assigned to VF-5A (later VF-51) for qualification aboard uss *Boxer* and familiarisation visits to other carriers.

*The FJ-1 Fury (NA-141) was North American's first jet fighter.*

With fighters of much higher performance already becoming available, however, the Navy reduced the FJ-1 contract from 100 to 30, and only the one unit was equipped with the type. The first carrier landings were made on March 10th, 1948, and the Fury subsequently became the first jet fighter to complete an operational tour at sea. It remained in front-line service for only fourteen months, however, before being assigned to US Naval Reserve units to make room for the Grumman Panther.

During the period of FJ-1 development, work had started on a similar straight-winged fighter for the USAAF, but this evolved into the swept-wing Sabre. In turn, the Sabre design was adopted by the Navy,

and although these aircraft were designated FJ-2, -3 and -4 and carried the name Fury, they really had little in common with the FJ-1, and are described separately.

## Specification (FJ-1)

| | |
|---|---|
| SPAN | 38ft 2in |
| LENGTH | 34ft 5in |
| HEIGHT | 14ft 10in |
| WING AREA | 221sq ft |
| GROSS WEIGHT | 15,600lb |
| MAX SPEED | 547mph at 9,000ft |
| RANGE (FERRY) | 1,496 miles |

## Production

*XFJ-1:* 39053 to 39055.
*FJ-1:* 120342 to 120371.

# F–86 Sabre, FJ Fury

Project designs for a high performance (subsonic) jet fighter for the USAAF were laid out by North American during 1944, alongside plans for a similar carrier-based fighter for the USN. The two designs were identified, respectively, as the NA–140 and NA–134 and the latter appeared in due course as the FJ–1 Fury, described separately. On May 18th, 1944, the USAAF ordered three prototypes of the NA–140 design, which had a General Electric J35 engine and a wing similar to that of the FJ–1 in planform but of thinner section, with a ten per cent thickness/chord ratio. With a span of 38ft 2½in, a length of 35ft 6in and a gross weight of 11,500lb, the NA–140 design, which the USAAF had designated XP–86, had an estimated maximum speed of 582mph at 10,000ft and a critical Mach number of 0·90. With auxiliary fuel tanks at each wing tip, the XP–86 had an estimated range of 750 miles.

A mock-up of the aircraft in this form was approved by the USAAF in June 1945 but as the estimated performance showed little advantage over the Republic P–84 which was already committed to production, North American engineers began an intensive study of the German data then becoming available to see whether the application of wing sweep-back would be advantageous. Wind tunnel testing in September was so encouraging that NAA submitted a revised, swept-wing version of the XP–86 design to the Air Force and this proposal was boldly accepted on November

*Early production F–86A (NA–151) Sabres awaiting delivery at Los Angeles.*

*F–86E (NA–170) Sabres.*

1st, 1945, establishing America's first swept-wing jet fighter firmly in development.

The revised design was completed and contractual details for the three prototypes worked out by June 20th, 1946, and the final go-ahead was given. Still using a J35 engine, the XP-86 now had sweepback of 35 degrees on the mainplane and swept-back tail surfaces, and with a design gross weight of 13,311lb, was expected to reach a top speed of 635mph at 16,000ft. A key feature of the design was the application of an automatic leading edge flap which opened at low speeds to improve the stability characteristics, but closed at high speeds to allow full advantage to be taken of the sweepback.

The first of the XP-86 prototypes flew at Muroc (now Edwards AFB) on October 1st, 1947, and a highly successful flight test programme was completed, in the course of which Mach 1 was exceeded for the first time on April 28th, 1948 (in a shallow dive). The XP-86 was thus the second American aeroplane to go supersonic and the first combat type to do so. With a 3,920lb st Allison J35-A-5 engine installed, the XP-86 demonstrated a top speed of

Top left: An F-86E (NA-170) Sabre with drop tanks incorporating refuelling probes.

Left: An F-86F (NA-172) over Korea.

Top right: The second TF-86F (NA-216) trainer, modified from an F-86F.

Right: An F-86H (NA-187) produced at the Columbus factory.

618mph in level flight at 14,000ft, flying at a take-off weight of 13,790lb. On November 28th, 1949, the first XP–86 made the first flight after installation of the 5,000lb st J35–A–17 engine.

Production of the new aeroplane—which was not named Sabre until March 1949 after it had entered squadron service—had been initiated in December 1946 with a letter contract for 33 P–86As. Subsequently the USAF ordered 190 P–86Bs, which were to have larger diameter wheels and a widened fuselage to accommodate the bigger wheel wells, but this contract was changed to cover 188 more P–86As and two P–86Cs, and 333 more P–86As were ordered in May 1948. The first P–86A flew on May 18th, 1948 and a month later the USAF changed its fighter designation category from 'P' to 'F', so henceforth the North American fighter was the F–86.

The F–86A was powered by the 4,850lb st General Electric J47–GE–1 engine and carried an armament of six 0·50in machine guns, three each side in the nose intake walls. Rockets, bombs or drop tanks could be carried beneath the wings on one pylon each side. This first version of the Sabre began to enter service with USAF fighter squadrons in February 1949, the first unit to fly the type being the 44th Squadron of the First Fighter Group—the famous 'Hat in the Ring' squadron. Five Wings of three squadrons each were eventually equipped with this model of the Sabre, and later several Air National Guard squadrons flew it. The Sabres of the 4th Fighter-Interception Wing were the first to see combat when they were deployed to Korea in December 1950 to counter the threat posed by the introduction of MiG–

15s, and several MiGs were destroyed in aerial combat before the end of the year.

The Korean war accounted for a rapid increase in Sabre production with the F–86E following the F–86A as the next TAC model. It differed from the F–86A only in having an all-flying tailplane and was first flown on September 23rd, 1950. Production totalled 396, of which sixty came from the production line established in Montreal by Canadair, primarily to build Sabres for the RCAF as described below. The F–86F, first flown on March 19th, 1952, differed from the E in having the 5,200lb st J47–GE–27 engine. Production of 235 F–86Fs (135 at Inglewood and 100 at Columbus) with one pylon under each wing, was followed by 1,459 more (859 Inglewood and 600 Columbus) with two pylons under each wing.

In the course of F–86F production, an important change was made to the wing configuration, a fixed leading edge replacing the original auto-slats. The new design increased the root chord by 6in and the tip chord by 3in, and was known as the '6–3' wing. All F–86Fs already produced were modified later to have the new wing, which improved the combat performance, in particular manoeuvrability at high altitude and high Mach number, at the expense of a higher landing speed. The final batch of 280 F–86Fs—built on USAF

Top right: *The first YF–93A (NA–157) with its original flush intake.*

Right: *Radar-equipped F–86D (NA–165) for Air Defence Command.*

72

contract to be supplied to Japan—had extended wing tips and leading edge slats, and these modifications were in turn introduced on many earlier F–86Fs in USAF service.

The versatility of the Sabre was further increased with production of the F–86H, first flown on April 30th, 1953. This model had a deepened fuselage to accommodate the 8,920lb st General Electric J73–GE–3 engine, wing span increased by two feet, enlarged tailplane with no dihedral and armament of four 20mm cannon in place of the six machine guns. (This armament had been tested in Korea in four F–86Es and eight F–86Fs). Internal fuel capacity was increased and the F–86H was equipped to serve in the fighter-bomber rôle. Production totalled 475, exclusively from Columbus after the first two examples from Inglewood.

In addition to the foregoing Sabre models for Tactical Air Command, an all-weather fighter version was developed for Air Defence Command as the F–86D. The major differences from the F–86A comprised installation of AN/APG–36 search radar in the nose above a redesigned air intake, and the use of an afterburner on the J47–GE–17 engine. First flight of the YF–86D (initially designated YF–95A) prototype was made on December 22nd, 1949, and production models began to

Top left: *An F–86L modification of the F–86D.*

Left: *An F–86K (NA–213) produced by North American for the Royal Netherlands Air Force.*

appear in March 1951 from Inglewood, where a total of 2,504 was built. The armament of this variant comprised twenty-four 2·75in air-to-air Folding Fin Aircraft Rockets in a retractable tray in the forward fuselage. Starting in 1956, 981 F–86Ds were converted to F–86L standard, with the extended wing of the F–86H, new leading-edge slats and a new avionics fit.

The F–86D was also adopted, in 1953, as a NATO all-weather interceptor, for production in Italy. Equipped with a new fire control system, this version was designated the F–86K. Two YF–86K prototypes were converted from F–86Ds, first flight being made on July 15th, 1954, and North American built 120 complete aircraft for Norway and Holland, plus 221 sets of parts for assembly by Fiat in Italy.

Non-production versions and other designations of the Sabre for the USAF and others included the following:

*F–86C:* Long-range fighter variant with larger overall dimensions, Pratt & Whitney J48–P–1 engine and fuselage-side intakes. Two prototypes built (first flight January 25th, 1950) after redesignation as YF–93A; production of 118 F–93As cancelled.

*F–86G:* Proposed designation of F–86D with J47–GE–33 engine. Production of 406 ordered, but redesignated F–86D–20 before delivery.

Top left: *A Marine Corps FJ–2 Fury (NA–181).*

Left: *An FJ–3 Fury (NA–194) in US Navy colours.*

*RF–86A:* A small number of F–86A conversions with three cameras in a bay beneath the cockpit.

*RF–86F:* Triple-camera conversions of F–86F, as RF–86A above.

*TF–86F:* Two F–86Fs converted to two-seat trainers by the extension of the fuselage by 5ft 3in. First flight December 14th, 1953.

In addition to its use by both TAC and ADC of the USAF, the Sabre was widely used by other air forces throughout the world. In several cases, substantial quantities of new F–86F Sabres were supplied direct to foreign users through the Mutual Air Program, the recipients including Japan (where Mitsubishi assembled 300 sets of parts from North American), Chinese Nationalist Republic, Belgium, Peru, Spain and Korea. The Fiat-built F–86Ks, the first of which was flown on May 23rd, 1955 at Turin, were supplied to the Air Forces of Italy, Germany and France, while F–86Ds, as they became surplus to USAF requirements, went to Denmark and Turkey. Many other nations, among them Venezuela, Portugal, Norway, Greece, Turkey, Pakistan, the Philippines, Thailand, Iraq and Yugoslavia received F–86Es, F–86Fs or F–86Hs from USAF surplus stock.

Additional Sabre production was undertaken in both Canada and Australia.

Top left: *The final Fury variant, a missile-armed FJ–4B (NA–244).*

Left: *Trial bipropellant rocket installation in an FJ–4F (NA–248).*

Canada acquired a license to build the F–86 in August 1949 and decided to substitute the locally-produced Avro Orenda engine. A trial installation was made in a North American-built F–86A (which was redesignated the F–86J) but the Orenda production timescale was such that initial Canadair production Sabres used the General Electric J47–GE–13. The first Canadair CL–13 to fly was an F–86A, called Sabre Mk 1 by the RCAF and flown at Dorval on August 9th, 1950, but production models with the J47 comprised 350 Sabre 2s and 438 Sabre 4s, the latter being produced primarily to meet RAF requirements. Of this total, sixty Mk 2s were purchased by the USAF and three Mk 2s and 427 Mk 4s went to the RAF, to serve as an interim fighter from 1952 to 1956 pending introduction of the Hunter. After being retired by the RCAF, many Canadair Sabre 2s were supplied to Greece and Turkey while many of the RAF Sabre 4s went to Italy and Yugoslavia. One of the RAF aircraft became a test-bed for the Bristol-Siddeley Orpheus engine.

The first Canadair-built Sabre with an Orenda was the single Mk 3. This was productionised as the Mk 5, of which 370 examples were built for the RCAF, 76 later being sold to the Luftwaffe. Whereas the Mk 5 had a 6,355lb st Orenda 10, the Sabre 6, which was the last Canadair

Top right: *The first Canadair-built Sabre 2 with Orenda engine.*

Right: *A Canadair Sabre 6 in RCAF service.*

production version, had the 7,275lb st Orenda 14. Production of this variant totalled 655, comprising 390 for the RCAF, six for Colombia, 34 for South Africa and 225 for Germany.

The Australian decision to build the Sabre was made in February 1951 and, as in Canada, use of an alternative power-plant was specified—in this case the Rolls-Royce Avon. Production was the responsibility of Commonwealth Aircraft Corporation, which built a prototype with an imported Avon R.A.7 as the CA–26, flown on August 3rd, 1953. The production model was the CA–27 with Australian-built Avon, Commonwealth building 21 Sabre 30s with Avon 20 engines and otherwise as the F–86E; 21 Sabre 31 with the '6–3' leading edge (plus most Sabre 30s converted) and 69 Sabre 32s with Avon 28, extra fuel capacity in the wings, dual store provision and capability to mount Sidewinder missiles.

Having ordered the FJ–1 Fury jet fighter into production before the Sabre appeared, the US Navy decided in 1951 to adopt a version of the USAF fighter, which offered better low-speed performance than some of the swept-wing designs already in Naval service. For maximum speed of production, the Navy specified the minimum changes from the F–86E, limiting these to the addition to deck-landing and catapult provisions. The new aircraft had virtually nothing in common with the FJ–1 Fury save the makers' name, but was designated as a new Fury variant so that the Navy did not have to justify to Congress the purchase of a completely new type of aircraft. Three prototypes were built at Inglewood, one XFJ–2B (the first to fly, on December 27th, 1951) with four 20mm cannon armament and two XFJ–2s with the standard Air Force armament of six 0·50in guns apiece. Powered by the 6,000lb st General Electric J47–GE–2 engine, the FJ–2 entered production at Columbus, 200 being built by September 1954.

Six US Marine Corps squadrons operated the FJ–2s, while Columbus went on to build 538 FJ–3s, powered by the 7,800lb st Wright J65–W–2 or 7,650lb st J65–W–4B engine, the US-built version of the Armstrong Siddeley Sapphire. The FJ–3 prototype flew on July 3rd, 1953 and the first production model appeared in December. More than twenty Navy and Marine squadrons operated the type.

The final Navy Fury variant was the FJ–4, which was a major redesign of the basic aircraft to allow it to carry fifty per cent more internal fuel without any loss of performance. The wing thickness/chord ratio was reduced from ten per cent to six per cent and the fuselage and fin contours changed. The first of two FJ–4 prototypes, with J65–W–4 engines, flew from Columbus on October 28th, 1954 and production models had the 7,700lb st J65–W–16A engine. A total of 152 was built, followed by 222 FJ–4Bs which had six instead of four wing pylons and were configured as ground-attack fighters.

Two FJ–4 Furies were tested in 1957 with rocket engines to boost their performance. The rocket was a North American AR–1, located in the tail above the jet pipe and burning hydrogen peroxide and JP–4. This installation proved highly unreliable and only a few test flights were made.

Non-production variants of the USN Fury were designated as follows:

*FJ–3M:* FJ–3s modified to have four under-wing pylons in place of two, and Sidewinder capability.
*FJ–3D:* Drone-control version for use with Vought Regulus missiles.
*FJ–3D–2:* Drone-control version for use with F9F–6K target drones.

When the uniform Navy/Air Force system of designations was introduced in 1962, the FJ–1 and FJ–2 were considered to have become the F–1A and F–1B respectively, although they were then out of service. In-service versions redesignated were the FJ–3 to F–1C; FJ–3M to MF–1C; FJ–3D to DF–1C; FJ–3D–2 to DF–1D; FJ–4 to F–1E and FJ–4B to AF–1E.

## Specification

|  | F–86A | F–86D | F–86E | F–86H | FJ–4 |
|---|---|---|---|---|---|
| SPAN | 37ft 1½in | 37ft 1½in | 37ft 1½in | 39ft 1½in | 39ft 1in |
| LENGTH | 37ft 6in | 40ft 3in | 37ft 6in | 38ft 10in | 36ft 4in |
| HEIGHT | 14ft 9in | 15ft | 14ft 9in | 14ft 11½in | 13ft 11in |
| WING AREA | 287·9sq ft | 287·9sq ft | 287·9sq ft | 313·4sq ft | 338·7sq ft |
| GROSS WEIGHT | 16,223lb | 19,975lb | 17,806lb | 24,296lb | 23,700lb |
| MAX SPEED (at sea level) | 679mph | 692mph | 679mph | 692mph | 680mph |
| CRUISING SPEED | 533mph | 550mph | 537mph | 552mph | 534mph |
| RANGE | 660 miles | 554 miles | 848 miles | 1,038 miles | 1,485 miles |

Commonwealth-built, Avon-powered Sabre 32 carrying Sidewinders.

## XSN2J–1

In 1945, the US Navy drew up requirements for a new scout trainer intended as a replacement for the SNJ Texan, and North American succeeded in winning a contract to build two prototypes of its NA–142 design. Powered by a 1,100hp Wright Cyclone R–1830–78 radial, the XSN2J–1 resembled the SNJ in general configuration but had considerably higher performance. It was equipped with arrester gear for carrier landing practice and for armament training it was fitted with two 0·50in machine guns and could carry bombs or rockets.

Two prototypes were built in 1946 and evaluated by the US Navy in conjunction with the Fairchild XNQ–1 primary trainer prototype, but the new training syllabus for which the two new types were intended was not in the event adopted. Features of the NA–142 design were revived by North American a little later in the NA–159 which, as the T–28B, was in due course adopted as the new Navy trainer combining the earlier primary and basic rôles.

### Specification

| | |
| --- | --- |
| SPAN | 42ft 11½in |
| LENGTH | 33ft 10in |
| HEIGHT | 14ft 7in |
| GROSS WEIGHT | 8,500lb |
| MAX SPEED | 270mph |
| CRUISING SPEED | 242mph |
| RANGE | 2,000 miles (with external tanks). |

### Production
121449 and 121450.

### Production
XP–86: 45–59597 to 45–59599.
F–86A: 47–605 to 47–637, 48–129 to 48–316, 49–1007 to 49–1339.
YF–86D: 50–577 to 50–578.
F–86D: 50–455 to 50–576, 50–704 to 50–734, 51–2944 to 51–3131, 51–5857 to 51–6262, 51–8274 to 51–8505, 52–3598 to 52–4304, 52–9983 to 52–10176, 53–557 to 53–1071, 53–3675 to 53–3710, 53–4018 to 53–4090.
F–86E: 50–579 to 50–689, 51–2718 to 51–2849, 51–12977 to 51–13069.
F–86E–CAN: 52–2833 to 52–2892, 52–10177 to 52–10236.
F–86F: 51–2850 to 51–2947, 51–12936 to 51–12976, 51–13070 to 51–13510, 52–4305 to 52–5530, 53–1072 to 53–1228, 55–3816 to 55–4030, 55–4983 to 55–5117, 56–2773 to 56–2882, 57–6338 to 57–6457.
YF–86H: 52–1975 to 52–1976.
F–86H: 52–1977 to 52–2124, 52–5729 to 52–5753, 53–1229 to 53–1528.

F–86K: 53–8273 to 53–8322, 54–1231 to 54–1350, 55–4881 to 55–4936, 56–4116 to 56–4160.
Sabre 1: 19101.
Sabre 2: 19102 to 19199, 19201 to 19452.
Sabre 3: 19200.
Sabre 4: 19453 to 19890.
Sabre 5: 23001 to 23370.
Sabre 6: 23371 to 23760, 2021 to 2026 (Colombia), 350 to 383 (South Africa), plus 225 for Luftwaffe.
CA–26 Sabre: A94–101.
CA–27 Sabre 30: A94–901 to A94–921.
CA–27 Sabre 31: A94–922 to A94–942.
CA–27 Sabre 32: A94–943 to A94–990, A94–351 to A94–371.
FJ–2: 133754 to 133756, 131927 to 132126.
FJ–3: 135774 to 136162, 139210 to 139278, 141364 to 141443.
FJ–4: 139279 to 139323, 139424 to 139530.
FJ–4B: 139531 to 139555, 141444 to 141489, 143493 to 143643.

*The first of two North American XSN2J-1s (NA-142).*

# Navion, L–17

For its first major civil aircraft venture, North American initiated, in the closing days of World War II, the design of an elegant low-wing four-seat lightplane. Reminiscent, in its somewhat angular outline, of the Mustang, the new monoplane was designed around a 185hp Continental engine and a mock-up was completed before the end of 1945, this design being the NA–143. The first of two prototypes was flying early in 1946, and large-scale production was launched immediately, the production version being the NA–145.

Sanguine expectations of the development of a mass market for light aircraft were not realised and by April 15th, 1947, North American had built 1,110 Navions but of these 280 were unsold. The company then decided to terminate production, and in June 1947 concluded an agreement for the outright sale of the design and manufacturing rights to Ryan Aeronautical Co.

From the existing stock, 83 Navions were sold to the US Army for use in the liaison rôle, being designated L–17A.

Subsequent to the sale of the Navion rights to Ryan, the type was developed through a succession of versions, first by Ryan and later by Navion Aircraft Corporation, which evolved the more powerful, five-seat Rangemaster. The US Army also bought from Ryan 163 Navions as L–17Bs, and 35 of the original North American aircraft were converted to L–17C with improved brakes and fuel tanks. The military designations were later changed to U–18A, U–18B and U–18C, the surviving aircraft being transferred to the USAF for use in AF aero clubs.

## Specification (Navion)

| | |
|---|---|
| SPAN | 33ft 4½in |
| LENGTH | 27ft 5¾in |
| HEIGHT | 8ft 7⅝in |
| WING AREA | 184sq ft |
| GROSS WEIGHT | 2,570lb |
| MAX SPEED | 160mph |
| CRUISING SPEED | 115mph |
| RANGE | 700 miles |

## Production
*NA–143:* NX18928, NX18929.
*L–17A:* 47–1297 to 47–1379 (plus NA–145 commercial production).

*Top left: A production model Navion lightplane (NA–145).*

*Left: One of 83 Navions supplied to the USAF as L–17As (NA–154).*

# AJ Savage

North American's first attack bomber for the US Navy was conceived in the period immediately following World War II, before the capabilities of jet propulsion had been fully appreciated. At the time, there appeared to be some merit in providing both piston engines and jet engines in a single airframe, and several Navy types of the period explored this configuration— the North American AJ–1 among them. The concept was for a high performance carrier-based bomber with nuclear capability, powered by two 2,400hp Pratt & Whitney R–2800–44W piston engines to obtain long-range cruise plus a 4,600lb st Allison J33–A–19 turbojet to boost speed over the target.

The NA–146 design that North American drew up to meet the Navy requirement featured a high wing (folding for carrier storage), single tail unit with dihedral on the tailplane and a crew of three. Three XAJ–1 prototypes (and a static test specimen) were ordered on June 24th, 1946, and the first of these, built at Inglewood, flew on July 3rd, 1948. Production of 48 examples of a similar version, the AJ–1, ensued, with deliveries starting in September 1949, the first squadron equipped being VC–5. Although some problems

Top right: *A production model AJ–1 (NA–160), showing dihedral on the tailplane.*

Right: *An AJ–2 (NA–184) adapted as a refuelling tanker.*

were encountered with the jet installation in the rear fuselage, the Savage provided the Navy with useful experience in handling large multi-engined aircraft aboard carrier decks, and production was continued with a total of 100 more in the AJ–2 and AJ–2P versions.

The 82 AJ–2s differed in having a taller fin and rudder assembly, no dihedral on the tailplane, slightly lengthened fuselage, more fuel, R–2800–48 and J33–A–10 engines and re-arranged cockpit to provide a single compartment, instead of two small ones, for the three-man crew. The first example flew on February 19th, 1953. The eighteen AJ–2Ps were similar but carried five reconnaissance cameras in a redesigned nose and other cameras and photo-flash bombs in the fuselage. First flight of this model was made on March 6th, 1952. Production of the Savage, which was undertaken in the Downey (AJ–1) and Columbus (AJ–2 and –2P) plants, was completed in the first half of 1954.

By 1959, the Savage had been replaced in the Navy's Attack squadrons, but many AJ–1s and AJ–2s were converted for use as flight refuelling tankers with a hose-and-reel unit in the bomb-bay. In the new rôle they were not redesignated, but in 1962 those aircraft still in service became A–2As and A–2Bs respectively. The AJ–2Ps were standard equipment of US Navy heavy photographic squadrons until the early 'sixties, when they were replaced by A3D Skywarriors.

## Specification (AJ–1 Savage)

| | |
|---|---|
| SPAN | 75ft 2in (over tip tanks) |
| LENGTH | 63ft 10in |
| HEIGHT | 20ft 5in |
| GROSS WEIGHT | 52,862lb |
| MAX SPEED | 471mph (all engines) |
| RANGE | 1,630 miles |

## Production

*XAJ–1:* 121460 to 121462.
*AJ–1:* 122590 to 122601, 124157 to 124186.
*AJ–2:* 124850 to 124864, 128043 to 128054, 130405 to 130421, 134035 to 134072.
*AJ–2P:* 129185 to 129195, 130422 to 130425, 134073 to 134075.

*AJ–2P (NA–175) reconnaissance versions of the Savage.*

# XA2J-1

Very few of the aircraft types developed by North American for the US Navy have failed to go into production, but the XA2J-1 (NA-163) was an exception. This large carrier-borne attack bomber originated in 1948 as a derivative of the AJ-1 Savage with turboprop engines, but following a mock-up review in September 1948, the US Navy ordered a series of major changes to be made in the two prototypes placed on order at that time. Further mock-up reviews were held in April and September 1949, modifications directed at that time including the deletion of the Allison J33 jet booster in the rear fuselage, as used in the Savage.

The power plant comprised two Allison XT40-A-6 turboprops in underwing nacelles, and each engine unit comprised a pair of T38 turboprops geared to drive contra-rotating propellers through a gearbox and clutch. This arrangement allowed either 'half' of the T40 to be stopped in cruising flight while the propeller assembly remained under power from the other half. A crew of three was carried in a pressurised compartment in the nose and the armament comprised two 20mm guns in a radar-controlled barbette. Maximum bomb-load was 10,500lb.

The first of two prototypes of the XA2J-1, built at the Inglewood plant, flew on January 4th, 1952, landing subsequently at Edwards AFB. Engine problems dogged the flight tests of this aircraft and the type was eventually abandoned in favour of jet-powered attack bombers of superior performance. The second prototype was completed but not flown, and a proposal to re-engine the XA2J-1 with Allison XT54-A-2 engines did not proceed.

## Specification

| | |
|---|---|
| SPAN | 71ft 6in |
| LENGTH | 70ft 2½in |
| HEIGHT | 22ft 5in |
| WING AREA | 853sq ft |
| GROSS WEIGHT | 58,000lb |
| MAX SPEED | 440mph |
| RANGE | 1,700 miles |

## Production

124439 and 124440.

*The prototype XA2J-1 (NA-163).*

# T–28 Trojan, Fennec, Nomad, Nomair

When the USAF initiated a design contest for a basic trainer to replace the T–6 Texan —which, as the NA–16, had played such a large part in establishing the reputation of North American—it was to be expected that the Inglewood company would spare no effort to design a worthy successor. With the NA–159 design, the company did in fact succeed in winning the contest, and gained a contract to build two prototypes in 1948. The designation XBT–28 had been reserved for the new basic trainer, but the 'BT' category was abandoned at about the time the NA–159 was ordered and the prototypes were built as XT–28s. The first flight was made on September 26th, 1949.

Principal differences between the XT–28 and the T–6 which it was destined to replace lay in the power—an 800hp Wright R–1300–1A engine made it one of the most powerful ab initio trainers ever projected—and in the tricycle undercarriage. Like the T–6, it had a low wing, single tail unit and tandem seating for pilot and instructor. Flight trials of the prototype confirmed the USAF's selection of the North American design and an initial contract was placed for 266 T–28As, the first of which was assigned as a static test specimen. Deliveries from Inglewood

*T–28A (NA–174) trainer for the USAF.*

84

began in 1950 and continued until 1953 by which time additional contracts brought total production for the USAF to 1,194. They remained in service at basic flight training schools until replaced by the jet-powered T–37A.

Following US Navy evaluation of two T–28As, a similar version was adopted by that service also, 489 being produced at Columbus as T–28Bs, starting in 1954. These had 1,425hp R–1820–86 engines and minor changes, while 299 T–28Cs for the Navy were distinguished by having arrester hooks to be used in dummy deck approach and landing training. The T–28C first flew on September 19th, 1955 and delivery of the last T–28C was made in 1957. One T–28B was also manufactured for Japan in 1954 when production of the type in Japan was under consideration by Mitsubishi.

When the USAF began to dispose of its T–28As, from 1958 onwards, several possible civilian uses for the type were explored. North American's Columbus division produced the NA–260 Nomad scheme, which introduced a 1,300hp Wright R–1820–56S engine and three-blade air-screw, and after converting a prototype, licensed Pacific Aeronautics Corporation to undertake further similar conversions. Hamilton Aircraft Co, Inc, of Tucson, Arizona, offered a similar engine installa-

Top right: *A Navy T–28B (NA–199)*.

Right: *T–28C (NA–252) with arrester hook for carrier approach training*.

tion in its T–28–R Nomair conversion, with the 1,200hp Wright 704C9GC1 as an alternative. A prototype was flown in September 1960 and a production model in February 1962, to provide the basis for FAA Type Approval. Two variants were offered—the T–28–R1 with two seats in tandem and the five-seat T–28–R2, with a fixed canopy and side door. Six T–28–R1s equipped with arrester hooks were supplied to the Brazilian Navy in 1962. A conversion of the T–28A for aerial photography duties was certificated in September 1958 by Thompson Aircraft Sales of Phoenix, Arizona.

The Pacair Nomad Scheme was adopted by the French Air Force in 1959 for use in the desert warfare and reconnaissance rôle in North Africa. The original Nomad conversion was shipped to France in July 1959 and three other conversions were supplied by Pac Aero, plus engineering assistance to allow Sud Aviation to convert a further 245 surplus USAF T–28As to the new standard at its St Nazaire plant. In addition to the engine change, the conversion included the provision under each wing of two bomb racks and a 12·5mm gun pod. In French service the type was known as the Fennec.

In 1961, the USAF began to acquire a similar armed conversion of the T–28A, primarily for use in Mutual Aid Programs

Top right: *An ex-USAF T–28A converted to armed Fennec configuration by Sud Aviation.*

Right: *T–28D conversions serving with the South Vietnamese Air Force.*

for other nations such as Congo, South Vietnam and South American countries. From then until early 1969, North American received 13 separate T–28 modification contracts to convert a total of 321 T–28As to T–28D configuration, and some T–28As to T–28Bs, and T–28Bs to T–28Cs. The T–28D procured by the USAF retained the original Wright R–1300 engine but had six underwing strong points plus two underwing guns and, in the T–28D–5 version, a total possible underwing load of 4,000lb. After the programme at Columbus ended, further contracts were placed with Fairchild's Republic Division to convert 72 more T–28As to T–28Ds.

A programme to develop a more potent counter-insurgency version of the T–28 was launched in 1962 when the USAF contracted with North American's Columbus Division for the conversion of two T–28As to YAT–28E standard (NA–284). This version had a 2,450hp Lycoming T55 turboprop and a strengthened wing with provision for twelve hardpoints in addition to two gun pods. The first aircraft (52–1242) flew on February 15th, 1963, but was lost on its fourteenth flight in March. The second aircraft was 51–3786 and a third conversion was ordered to replace the first. This third aircraft (51–3788) flew in July 1964 and had additional modifications, including ejection seats for both occupants

*The first YAT–28E (NA–284) conversion.*

and a higher canopy. No production of the YAT–28E took place.

## Specification (T–28)

| | |
|---|---|
| SPAN | 40ft 1in |
| LENGTH | 32ft |
| HEIGHT | 12ft 8in |
| WING AREA | 268sq ft |
| GROSS WEIGHT | 8,000lb (T–28A) |
| | 8,584lb (T–28B) |
| | 8,350lb (Nomad) |
| MAX SPEED | 283mph at 5,800ft (T–28A) |
| | 345mph at 18,000ft (T–28B) |
| | 353mph at 18,000ft (Nomad) |
| CRUISING SPEED | 190mph (T–28A) |
| | 218mph (T–28B) |
| | 202mph (Nomad) |
| RANGE | 1,050 miles (T–28A) |
| | 905 miles (T–28B) |
| | 1,182 miles (Nomad) |

## Production

*XT–28:* 48–1371 to 48–1372.
*T–28A:* 49–1491 to 49–1756, 50–195 to 50–319, 51–3463 to 51–3796, 51–7482 to 51–7891, 52–1186 to 52–1242, 52–3497 to 52–3498.
*T–28B:* 137638 to 137810, 138103 to 138367, 140002 to 140052.
*T–28C:* 140053 to 140077, 140449 to 140666, 146238 to 146293.

Top right: *Third and last of the YAT–28Es, showing the additional wing hardpoints.*

Right: *North American's Nomad conversion of the T–28 (NA–260).*

# F–100 Super Sabre

Derived, as its name suggested, from the F–86 Sabre, the F–100 Super Sabre was the first truly supersonic fighter to enter service anywhere in the world. Whereas the Sabre and several of its swept-wing contemporaries could exceed the speed of sound in a dive, the Super Sabre could sustain speeds of up to Mach 1·3 in level flight. Its 'F–100' destination was no more than coincidence but as a result it was known as the first of the 'Century' series of fighters which, because of their supersonic capability, represented a new operational phase for the USAF.

Design work on a Sabre development began as a private venture in February 1949, and with a wing sweep-back angle of 45 deg this project became known as the Sabre 45. It was designed around a Pratt & Whitney J57 turbojet and resembled the Sabre only in general configuration and structural design. The appearance of the MiG–15 over Koera strengthened the USAF's interest in the new design and in November 1951 an order was placed for two prototypes (NA–180) and a production run of 110 aircraft, the designation F–100 being allocated at this time.

The YF–100A prototypes were first flown on May 25th and October 14th, 1953, respectively, and were powered by XJ57–

*Top right: An F–100C (NA–217) Super Sabre.*

*Right: F–100D (NA–223) in service with the Royal Danish Air Force.*

P–7 turbojets. The first production F–100A, with a 9,300lb st J57–P–7, flew on October 29th, 1953, and production built up rapidly to allow activation of the first Super Sabre unit in Tactical Air Command, the 479th Fighter Day Wing, to begin in September 1954. To overcome a serious control defect, a larger fin and rudder was introduced after seventy F–100As had been delivered, and the wing span was slightly increased. Later aircraft had the J57–P–39 engine.

The F–100A, armed with four 20mm M–39E cannon in the forward fuselage and missiles or other stores on six points under the wings, operated primarily as a day fighter. After delivery of 203 examples, production switched to the F–100C, primarily a fighter-bomber with strengthened wing structure to carry up to 7,500lb of stores on eight pylons, and increased internal fuel capacity in wing tanks. The first F–100C flew at Los Angeles on January 17th, 1955, after a modified F–100A had served as a prototype, and a second production source was established at the Columbus factory, where the first F–100C–10–NH flew on September 8th, 1955. All but the first few had J57–P–21

Top left: *Two F–100D (NA–223) Super Sabres demonstrate 'buddy' flight refuelling.*

Left: *An F–100D (NA–225) demonstrates zero-length take-off from inside a hangar using a rocket engine booster.*

Right: *A two-seat F–100F (NA–243).*

*The NF–100F used for low-speed research, with a special thrust reverser and other modifications.*

engines. Production totals were 451 and 25 from the Los Angeles and Columbus lines respectively.

Operational experience and design refinement led to further improvements in the F–100D, first flown at Los Angeles on January 24th, 1956. There was a further increase in vertical tail area, inboard landing flaps were introduced and the underwing pylons were made jettisonable. Production totals were 940 from Los

Angeles and 334 from Columbus, where the first example flew on June 12th, 1956.

A two-seat operational training version of the Super Sabre was first flown on August 6th, 1956, with the designation TF–100C, this version (a converted F–100C) having only two 20mm cannon, and the fuselage lengthened by 36in to accommodate the extra cockpit. It was productionised as the F–100F, first flown on March 7th, 1957, and continuing in

production until October 1959, by which time 339 had been built at the Los Angeles plant.

During its service life, the Super Sabre went through several development programmes and new equipment was progressively added. A technique of zero-launching, using a 150,000lb thrust Astrodyne rocket and an elevated ramp, was demonstrated successfully and all F–100Ds were fitted for this type of launching if required. A tail hook was also added, for use with runway arrester systems. A flight-refuelling probe was an earlier addition, and Bullpup ASM missiles were cleared for installation later.

At its peak, the Super Sabre equipped a total of sixteen USAF wings, and four of these saw service in Vietnam, starting in 1966 and ending in 1971. During this period, F–100s flew hundreds of thousands of missions and proved to be among the most versatile of tactical fighters in the theatre. Several other nations also used the Super Sabre, including the Chinese Nationalist Air Force, which between 1960 and 1970 received eighty F–100As updated to F–100D standard; the Turkish Air Force, which received 260 F–100Cs and a few F–100Fs; the Danish Air Force, which operated three squadrons of F–100Ds and used a few F–100Fs; and the French Air Force, which had two wings equipped with F–100Ds. Examples of the Super Sabre were still serving with the USAF and the Chinese, Turkish and Danish Air Forces in 1972.

Other experimental and projected versions included the following:

*F–100B:* An uprated development which

became the F–107, described separately.

*DF–100F:* Drone or missile director, conversions from F–100F.

*NF–100F:* One F–100F (56–3725) fitted with a Rohr thrust reverser, larger air-brake, blown flaps and other modifications for a low-speed research programme.

*F–100J:* Proposed for sale to Japan.

*F–100L:* Proposed with J57–P–55 engine.

*F–100N:* Proposed simplified version of F–100D.

*F–100S:* Proposed two-seat version for production in France, with Rolls-Royce RB168–25R Spey turbofan engine.

## Specification

| | |
|---|---|
| SPAN | 38ft 9in |
| LENGTH (excluding nose probe) | 47ft (F–100D) 50ft (F–100F) |
| HEIGHT | 16ft 2¾in |
| WING AREA | 385sq ft |
| GROSS WEIGHT | 34,832lb |
| MAX SPEED | 864mph at 35,000ft |
| CRUISING SPEED | 565mph |
| RANGE | 1,500 miles |

## Production

*YF–100A:* 52–5754 to 52–5755.

*F–100A:* 52–5756 to 52–5778, 53–1529 to 53–1708.

*F–100C–NA:* 53–1709 to 53–1778, 54–1740 to 54–2120.

*F–100C–NH:* 55–2709 to 55–2733.

*F–100D–NA:* 54–2121 to 54–2303, 55–3502 to 55–3814, 56–2903 to 56–3346.

*F–100D–NH:* 55–2734 to 55–2954, 56–3351 to 56–3463.

*F–100F:* 56–3725 to 56–4019, 58–1205 to 58–1233, 58–6975 to 58–6983, 59–2558 to 59–2563.

# F–107 and F–108

An extensive redesign of the basic F–100 Super Sabre was undertaken soon after the type had been put into production, with the object of providing a tactical fighter-bomber optimised for its ground attack capability. The initial study was designated F–100B, but when the Air Force ordered prototypes, the designation changed to YF–107A.

The YF–107A (NA–212) was powered by the 24,500lb thrust (with afterburner) Pratt & Whitney J75–P–9 turbojet, and to permit installation of a fire control radar in the nose, the air intake was relocated to a dorsal position behind the cockpit. Armament comprised four 20mm M–39E cannon and up to 10,000lb of stores could be carried beneath the wings and recessed under the fuselage. The three prototypes completed (six more being cancelled) made their first flights, respectively, on September 10th, November 28th and December 10th, 1956, but the YF–107As were not successful in winning Air Force approval and little

*The first F–107A (NA–212) showing semi-recessed fuel tank.*

development flying was completed on the type.

Although the Super Sabre continued in production for several more years, the YF–107 was the last fighter built by North American for the USAF. The greatly more ambitious F–108 (NA–257) Rapier designed as Weapon System 202 for a long-range Mach 3 interceptor for Air Defense Command and powered by two General Electric J93–GE–3 turbojets, continued in design and development until September 1959 when it, too, was cancelled (before completion of a prototype)—a sacrifice on the altar to guided missiles. A major effort was made by North American Rockwell to re-enter the fighter field with a design for the USAF's F–15 programme, but in a final competition the NR design lost out to that offered by McDonnell Douglas. The company was more successful, however, in the design competition for a new V/STOL fighter to serve aboard the US Navy's proposed sea control ships and in October 1972 received a contract to build two prototypes.

**Specification (F–107)**

| | |
|---|---|
| SPAN | 36ft 7in |
| LENGTH | 60ft 10in |
| HEIGHT | 19ft 8in |

**Production**
*YF–107A:* 55–5118 to 55–5120.

Top left: *Second F–107A with dummy bomb under fuselage.*

Left: *The third and last F–107A, showing the dorsal intake.*

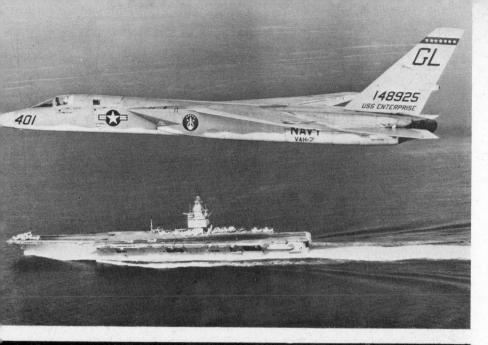

## A–5 Vigilante

Conception of the Vigilante, one of the largest and heaviest aircraft ever accepted for service aboard US Navy carriers, was closely related to American nuclear deterrent policies in the 'fifties. To help provide its share of the deterrent, the US Navy wanted a long-range carrier-launched bomber which could carry nuclear or conventional bombs. In response to the official requirement, North American proposed its NA–233 design for a two-seat attack bomber, projected at the Columbus Division and known initially as the NAGPAW —North American General Purpose Attack Weapon.

This design was accepted by the Navy in June 1956 and a contract for two prototypes designated YA3J–1 was confirmed in August. Production was launched under the company designation NA–247 and continued with later charge numbers as listed in the appendix. The new Navy bomber was named Vigilante in due course, and the designation changed in 1962 to A–5. Powered by two General Electric YJ79–GE–2 engines along each side of the rear fuselage, with variable-geometry intakes and the crew of two in tandem in the front fuselage. Between the engine jet pipes was a so-called linear bomb-bay—a slender tube-like cell in which the bomb or bombs were carried on rails. Bombs were catapult-

Top left: *An A–5A (NA–269) over the USS Enterprise.*

Left: *One of the few A–5Bs (NA–269) before modification to RA–5C standard.*

launched through the end of this cell, in the rear fuselage; two fuel tanks were also carried in the bomb-bay and, being emptied first, were ejected with the bomb and used to stabilise it during the fall. Another unusual feature of the Vigilante was the use of blown flaps, using engine-bleed air.

First flight of the prototype was made at Columbus on August 31st, 1958, and the first operational unit, VAH–7, began to form with Vigilantes in mid-1961. Production A–5As were powered by J79–GE–2, –4 or –8 engines and had provision for underwing fuel on two pylons. Production totalled 57 plus the two prototypes. VAH–1 and VAH–3 also flew this type.

Design improvements were planned for subsequent production Vigilantes, which were ordered by the US Navy as A3J–2 and A3J–3P (later A–5B and RA–5C respectively). In the A–5B, which was first flown on April 29th, 1962, additional fuel was carried in the forward fuselage, resulting in a pronounced hump behind the cockpit. Other changes included flaps of greater span and blowing of the leading edge flaps, as well as the trailing edge flaps. Two more wing pylons were fitted, and all four could carry 400-US gallon drop tanks. The same new features were to be applied to the RA–5C, which retained the same weapon capability but had

extensive tactical reconnaissance equipment including frame and panoramic cameras, side-looking radar and passive electronic countermeasures gear contained in a long fairing under the fuselage.

Before the A–5B could be introduced into service, the US shifted the emphasis of its defence strategy and the US Navy relinquished the strategic nuclear bombing rôle. Consequently, production was switched to the RA–5C after only six A–5Bs had been built. The first RA–5C flew on June 30th, 1962 and squadron service with this variant began two years later when RVAH–5 took its aircraft aboard USS *Ranger*. After production of

*An RA–5C (NA–269) showing the sensor pod beneath the fuselage.*

RA–5Cs ended, the US Navy contracted with Columbus Division to convert a total of 59 of the earlier aircraft to RA–5C configuration, starting in 1964, and the combined programmes provided enough aircraft for at least nine squadrons to equip with the type.

The continuing need for combat aircraft in the Vietnam war led to additional contracts for 46 RA–5Cs being placed in 1968, these being to a new standard with 11,870lb st J79–GE–10 engines, revised intakes and new nacelle–to–wing fillets. These changes were tested on a converted RA–5C from the earlier batch and the first of the new aircraft flew in March 1969.

In 1971, a derivative of the A–5C design with a third J79 in the rear fuselage was projected, as NR–349, to meet USAF Aerospace Defense Command's need for an Improved Manned Interceptor (IMI).

### Specification (RA-5C)

| | |
|---|---|
| SPAN | 53ft |
| LENGTH | 75ft 10in |
| HEIGHT | 19ft 5in |
| WING AREA | 769sq ft |
| GROSS WEIGHT | 80,000lb |
| MAX SPEED | 1,380mph at 40,000ft (approx) |
| CRUISING SPEED | 1,250mph |
| RANGE | 3,000 miles |

### Production

*XA3J–1:* 145157 to 145158.
*A–5A:* 146694 to 146702, 147850 to 147863, 148924 to 148933, 149276 to 149299.
*A–5B:* 149300 to 149305.
*RA–5C:* 149306 to 149317, 150823 to 150842, 151615 to 151634, 151726 to 151728, 151962 to 151969, 156608 to 156653.

## B–70 Valkyrie

The most controversial of all North American aeroplanes, and technically one of the company's most significant achievements to date, was the XB–70 supersonic bomber. Launched as a project to replace the Boeing B–52 as America's primary deterrent force, the B–70 was overtaken by changing defence policies and escalating costs and only two prototypes were built in what was probably the most expensive aerospace programme ever in relation to units flown.

The project began formally on October 14th, 1954, when USAF HQ issued its GOR 38 'General Operational Requirement for an Intercontinental Bombardment Weapon System Piloted Bomber'. The aircraft was to be all-chemical-fuelled and was expected to be in the active Strategic Air Command inventory in the period 1965–1975, with a target introduction date for the first thirty aircraft of 1963. Issue of the GOR came after some two years of USAF, NASA and industry studies of the feasibility of such a weapon system, which was initially for an aircraft with a Mach 0·9 cruise and supersonic dash capability for a 1,000 mile penetration of enemy airspace. By the time the prototypes were launched, however, the aircraft was designed to

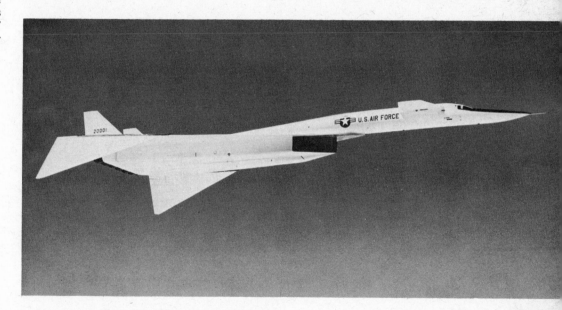

*The first XB–70A (NA–278), showing downturned wing tips.*

*Second XB-70A at take-off, with wing tips spread.*

maintain a supersonic cruise at all times, with a top speed of Mach 3.

Boeing and North American competed for the contract, the latter being selected winner in December 1957. The initial design studies had been launched at Los Angeles as NA-239 on September 12th, 1955, and constantly changing USAF directives took the project through NA-259, NA-264, NA-267 and NA-274 to NA-278, which covered three prototypes ordered on October 4th, 1961. The weapons system designation was WS110A for the bomber, which became the B-70; a reconnaissance version was also considered as WS110L but was dropped in July 1956. Some five years later, the strategic reconnaissance version was resurrected, as the RS-70, when the USAF was seeking to retain the programme in the face of mounting

opposition to the whole concept of a supersonic unarmed bomber force. However, the third prototype was deleted on May 3rd, 1964, and construction of two XB-70As was allowed to proceed only as a research programme.

The B-70, named Valkyrie by North American, was an advanced aerodynamic design of delta-wing layout with a foreplane and hinged wing tips that could be folded down to a 65 degree angle to enhance stability at supersonic speed. The design made use of compression lift theories to allow the B-70 to 'ride on its own shock wave' at Mach 3. Advanced structural design and many new techniques were required to allow the B-70 to tolerate the high temperatures derived from skin friction at high speeds.

Planned powerplant comprised, initially,

six General Electric J93-GE-5 turbojets with afterburners, using high-energy fuel. Development of this engine was cancelled when it was eventually calculated that the mission performance could be achieved without using HEF, and J93-GE-3 engines were substituted. In the prototypes, YJ93-GE-3 engines were rated at 30,000lb thrust each and were located behind a complex air intake control system with fixed and variable ramps.

Finished overall in gleaming white, the first XB-70A rolled out on May 11th, 1964, and was flown for the first time on September 21st from Palmdale, the pilots being North American's Alvin S. White and the USAF's Col Joseph F. Cotton. A concentrated flight test programme was conducted with no major setbacks and Mach 3 was reached for the first time on October 14th,

1965. The second XB–70A, incorporating many improvements and refinements, was first flown on July 17th, 1965, reached Mach 3 on January 3rd, 1966 and sustained that speed for 32 minutes on May 19th. However, the second aircraft was tragically lost after being struck by an escorting Lockheed F–104A during an air-to-air photographic sortie on June 8th, 1966 when only 46 flights had been made.

Flight testing of the first XB–70A continued at a relatively slow rate, since this aircraft had certain limitations that had been 'designed out' in the second aircraft. Responsibility for testing was assumed by NASA in March 1967 and some test programmes were completed in connection with the US SST project. The XB–70A made its last flight on February 4th, 1969, when it was ferried across the US to Wright Paterson AFB, Ohio, for inclusion in the Air Force Museum. This final flight was the 83rd made by the first prototype, the longest flight made by either prototype and the only time either aircraft had landed away from Edwards AFB. The entire programme was reported to have cost over $2,000million to design and build the two prototypes, and each test flight was said to cost $800,000.

## Specification (XB–70)

| | |
|---|---|
| SPAN | 105ft |
| LENGTH | 196ft |
| HEIGHT | 30ft |
| WING AREA | 6,297sq ft |
| GROSS WEIGHT | 550,000lb |
| MAX SPEED | 2,000mph |

## Production
*XB–70:* 62–001 and 62–207.

# X–15

Of the family of 'X' research aeroplanes built in America since 1945, the most remarkable was the hypersonic X–15. The series of flights made by three X–15s between 1959 and 1969 achieved speeds and altitudes unmatched by any manned aircraft designed to operate within the earth's atmosphere, as distinct from spacecraft. No other single aerospace research programme contributed so much information of vital use in the development both of high performance aircraft and of space vehicles.

The initiative for development of a research aircraft capable of reaching a speed of 6,600 ft/sec (about Mach 6) and an altitude of 250,000ft was taken by NACA during 1954, with an agreed programme in which the USAF and Navy would finance prototypes, with the USAF administering design and construction and the NACA having overall technical direction. It was assumed from the outset that the aircraft would be air-launched from a mother-plane (like the Bell X–1 and X–2 and Douglas D–558–II) and would be rocket-powered.

Twelve prospective contractors were invited on December 30th, 1954, to submit proposals and on February 4th, 1955, four prospective engine manufacturers were asked to submit engine proposals. Evaluation of the proposals led to selection of the

*A view of the first of the X–15A (NA–240) research craft, the fastest manned aeroplane yet built.*

North American NA–240 design, a letter contract being awarded on November 18th, 1955, and Reaction Motors Inc was selected as the engine supplier in September 1956.

North American's design team for this major assignment was headed by Harrison Storms with Charles Feltz as project engineer. The need to air-launch the X–15 at an altitude where the rocket-engine would boost it into a sub-orbital flight imposed severe restrictions on the design team—the only possible mother-craft were the Convair B–36 or the Boeing B–52, effectively limiting the length to about 50ft and gross weight to about 30,000lb. Two Boeing B–52s were in due course adopted as carriers, the X–15 being slung beneath the starboard wing inboard of the engines; these two aircraft, originally a B–52A and RB–52B, became the NB–52A and NB–52B respectively.

The X–15 evolved during 1956 as a mid-wing monoplane having a long tubular body with side fairings containing control runs and propellent. The tail unit was cruciform, provision being made for the ventral fin to be jettisoned shortly before touch down, which was made on twin nosewheels and twin steel skids under the rear fuselage, all units of this landing gear being retractable. Numerous design problems were encountered and overcome to

Top left: *The first X–15A leaving its NB–52A mother-ship; the complete ventral fin is shown fitted.*

Left: *The third X–15A installed beneath the wing of the NB–52.*

produce an aeroplane capable of withstanding unprecedentedly high skin temperatures and which could be controlled at speeds four times greater than any achieved at the time the X–15 was designed.

Three prototypes were ordered from North American, and while work proceeded on the ultimate rocket engine for the project, which was to give 57,000lb thrust for ninety seconds, it was decided to fit the first two X–15As with a pair each of the XLR–11 engines, giving a combined thrust of 16,000lb. The first X–15A, with these engines, was rolled out on October 15th, 1958, and moved from Los Angeles to Edwards AFB, from where the first flight beneath a B–52 was made on March 10th, 1959. It was not released on this flight and several more captive flights were made before the first release, on June 8th, 1959, for an unpowered flight with NAA test pilot Scott Crossfield at the controls. Meanwhile the second X–15A had been completed, and in this aircraft Scott Crossfield made the first powered flight of an X–15, on September 17th, 1959, reaching Mach 2·1. The first powered flight in the first X–15A was made on January 23rd, 1960.

The definitive XLR–99 engine was fitted from the outset in the third X–15A, but during preliminary ground runs this aircraft was severely damaged and the first flight of the new engine was made in the second X–15A on November 15th, 1960. The first prototype re-engined with the XLR99, rejoined the programme on August 11th, 1961, and the third X–15A, rebuilt and fitted with an adaptive control system, made its first flight later in the same year. Between then and 1963, the three X–15As progressively reached out to the limits of their design envelope, achieving a maximum speed of 4,104mph, Mach number of 6·06, altitude of 354,200ft (67 miles)

*One of the X–15As showing the landing skids deployed, with the lower ventral fin removed.*

and skin temperature of 1,320° F. The third aircraft was eventually lost in a landing accident on November 15th, 1967.

Earlier, on November 9th, 1962, the second X-15 had been damaged in an accident, and it was then rebuilt with modifications designed to permit even higher speeds to be achieved. Modifications included lengthening the fuselage by 29in, adding external fuel tanks and providing an external ablative coating to help protect the aeroplane from high temperatures. In this modified form, and still with the XLR99–RM–2 rocket engine, the X–15A–2 first flew on June 28th, 1964 and on October 3rd, 1967, this aircraft reached a new high speed of Mach 6·72 or 4,534mph. The test programme was concluded in 1968 with just under 200 flights made by the three aircraft.

## Specification (X–15)

| | |
|---|---|
| SPAN | 22ft |
| LENGTH | 50ft (X–15A) |
| | 52ft 5in (X15A–2) |
| HEIGHT | 13ft 6in |
| WING AREA | 200sq ft |
| GROSS WEIGHT | 34,000lb (X–15A) |
| | 50,914lb (X–15A–2) |
| MAX SPEED | 4,159mph (X–15A) |
| | 4,250mph (X–15A–2) |

## Production
X–15–1: 56–6670.
X–15–2: 56–6671.
X–15–3: 56–6672.

*Left: The rebuilt X–15A–2 with long-endurance fuel tanks and added protection against high temperatures.*

# T–2 Buckeye

With its NA–241 design, North American's Columbus Division was successful in meeting a US Navy requirement for a basic jet trainer. In common with many other Services around the world, the Navy was seeking a single aircraft capable of fulfilling a broad spectrum of training duties, taking students who had completed an ab initio course through all subsequent stages up to carrier qualification.

For speed of development and low cost, North American adopted proven design features wherever possible, basing the NA–241 upon the wing of the FJ–1 Fury, with the control system based on that of the T–28C. The crew were seated in tandem on zero-level ejection seats specially developed for the aircraft by the Columbus Division. Bifurcated intakes were provided for a single 3,400lb st Westinghouse J34–WE–36 jet engine located in the underside of the fuselage and the aircraft was designed for carrier operation and with capability to carry weapons under the wings for armament training.

Design of the NA–241 was initiated in June 1956 and the Navy backed the North American effort with a contract for six aircraft. The first of two were completed as XT2J–1 prototypes, first flight being made at Columbus by Dick Wenzell on January 31st, 1958. Production orders followed and, after carrier qualification trials aboard the USS *Antietam* in May 1959, deliveries of T2J–1s began in July the same year. The name Buckeye, selected for the new trainer, is the nickname of the state of Ohio, where it is built. The designation was changed to T–2A in 1962.

Production of the T–2A totalled 217, the primary users being squadrons of the Naval Air Basic Training Command—VT–7 and VT–9 with sixty aircraft each at NAAS Meridian, Miss, and VT–4 (for gunnery and carrier qualification training) at Sherman Field, NAS Pensacola, Florida.

Two years after production of the T–2A ended, North American developed a new version in which two 3,000lb st Pratt & Whitney J60–P–6 engines replaced the single J34. Two T2J–1s were converted to XT2J–2 prototypes (later YT–2B) in this configuration as NA–280, the first flight being made on August 30th, 1962. Produc-

*A T–2A (NA–253) Buckeye in the USN's red-and-white trainer finish.*

tion contracts for 97 T–2Bs followed, with the first flight on May 21st, 1965 and deliveries to VT–7 and VT–9 starting one year later. After the first 33 T–2Bs had been built, a production change was made to add 100 US gal of fuel in wing leading edge tanks, and to fit longer undercarriage legs.

The third production series of Buckeyes resulted from substitution of 2,950lb st General Electric J85 engines for the J60s. The last three contracted T–2Bs were completed to this new T–2C standard, first flight being made on April 17th, 1968. Production contracts for 144 followed, with the first flight of a production T–2C being made on December 10th, 1968 and production continuing into 1973. The T–2D designation referred to 12 Buckeyes ordered for the Venezuelan Air Force in 1972.

During 1970, North American received a contract from NASA to fit a supercritical wing on a T–2C. This project involved modifying a standard wing to have a thicker section with a flat top surface. The first flight was made by Ed Gillespie at Columbus at the end of November 1970.

**Specification (T–2C)**

| | |
|---|---|
| SPAN | 38ft 1½in |
| LENGTH | 38ft 3½in |
| HEIGHT | 14ft 9½in |
| WING AREA | 255sq ft |
| GROSS WEIGHT | 13,179lb |
| MAX SPEED | 521mph at 25,000ft |
| RANGE | 1,070 miles |

**Production**

*XT2J–1:* 144217/144218.
*T–2A:* 144219/144222, 145996/146015, 147430/147530, 148150/148239.
*T–2B:* 152382/152391, 152440/152475, 153538/153555, 155206/155238.
*T–2C:* 155239/155241, 156686/156733, 157030/157065, 158310/158333.

# Sabreliner

Design of the Sabreliner began in March 1956 as the NA–246, being a small jet transport for military or civil use. The prototype was built to compete for a USAF contract which was offered for an 'off-the-shelf' design subject to satisfactory evaluation; the requirement was known as the UTX (utility and 'combat readiness' trainer) and was announced in August 1956. The NA–246 design featured a low, swept-back wing, swept-back tail unit and engine pods on each side of the rear fuselage aft of the cabin, which seated up to eight passengers in addition to the two pilots.

Powered by two 2,500lb st General Electric YJ85 turbojets, the prototype flew at Los Angeles on September 16th, 1958, and following USAF evaluation the type was selected to fill the UTX rôle. After the bulk of military contracts had been met, the Sabreliner was offered on the commercial market as an executive jet, and its success in this field led to the development of several improved models.

The military versions were as follows:

*T–39A:* The basic USAF utility trainer, powered by two 3,000lb st Pratt & Whitney J60–P–3 turbojets (first six delivered with YJ60–P–1 engines) and differing from the prototype in having a lengthened nose and more complete equipment. First flown on June 30th, 1960 and a total of 143 built for the USAF.
*T–39B:* Six aircraft for USAF similar to T–39A but with R–14 NASARR search and ranging radar and APN–131 Doppler, for use in training F–105 crews. Operated

*The second prototype YT–2B (NA–280) showing the twin jet pipes.*

at Nellis AFB from February 1961, and later at McConnell AFB.

*T–39C:* Designation reserved for projected version equipped to train SAC ECM and radar operators.

*T–39D:* US Navy version similar to T–39B but with APQ–94 interceptor radar to permit their use in radar training of F–8 and F–4 crews. Procured as T3J–1s, but redesignated before deliveries began in August 1963. Total of 42 acquired.

*CT–39E:* Examples of commercial Sabreliner 40, powered by JT12A–8 engines, acquired by US Navy for use for rapid response airlift of high priority passengers, ferry pilots and cargo. Nine ordered up to 1972.

*T–39F:* Three T–39As converted for use at the USAF Fighter Weapons School at Nellis AFB to train electronic warfare officers and pilots for the F–105G equipped with Wild Weasel 3 ECM equipment.

To meet the original USAF requirements, the Sabreliner had to be certified to full commercial standards, this process being put in hand in December 1959. The first type approval was obtained on March 23rd, 1962, for the T–39A and the T–39B and T–39D were approved later the same year, the designations for certification purposes being NA–265, NA–265–20 and NA–265–30 respectively.

When a purely commercial model was produced (NA–282) it was more con-

*Top right: The original NA–246 Sabreliner, built primarily to meet a USAF requirement.*

*Right: A USAF T–39A Sabreliner (NA–265).*

veniently certificated as a variant of the original NA–265, becoming the NA–265–40, approved on April 17th, 1963. Consequently, the first commercial model became the Sabreliner Series 40, and subsequent variants continued this sequence of designation, as listed below. Nearly 200 commercial Sabreliners had been sold by 1972.

*Sabreliner 40:* The basic commercial model powered by 3,000lb st Pratt & Whitney JT12A–6A engines and with accommodation for up to ten passengers. Distinguished from early military models by having three cabin windows instead of two each side. Name changed to Sabre Commander 40A in 1971.

*Sabreliner 50:* A single aircraft built as an electronic equipment test-bed for use by North American Autonetics Division, with same basic airframe as Sabreliner 40.

*Sabreliner 60:* Certificated in April 1967 with 3,300lb st JT12A–8 or –8A engines and increased gross weight of 20,000lb. Fuselage lengthened by 3ft 2in; five cabin windows each side.

*Sabreliner 70:* First flown on December 4th, 1969 and certificated in June 1970. As Sabreliner 60 but with deepened fuselage cross-section, square cabin windows and other improvements. Name changed to Sabre 75 in 1971.

*Sabre 75A:* Succeeded Sabre 75 in 1972, with 4,315lb. st CF700–20–2 engines. First flight on October 18th, 1972.

Top right: *An early Sabreliner executive model, (NA–282), with only two cabin windows.*

Right: *A Sabreliner 60 (NA–306), left, and a late production Sabreliner 40 (NA–290).*

*Sabreliner 80:* Proposed version with Garrett AiResearch ATF 3 turbofans, abandoned in 1972.

## Specification

| | |
|---|---|
| SPAN | 44ft 5¼in (all models) |
| LENGTH | 43ft 9in (except Srs 75) |
| | 47ft (Srs 75) |
| HEIGHT | 16ft (except Srs 75) |
| | 17ft 6½in (Srs 75) |
| WING AREA | 342·6sq ft (all models) |
| GROSS WEIGHT | 17,760lb (T–39A) |
| | 18,650lb (Srs 40) |
| | 20,000lb (Srs 60) |
| | 21,200lb (Srs 75) |
| MAX SPEED | 563mph (Srs 60) |
| CRUISING SPEED | 475mph (T–39A) |
| | 461mph (Srs 40) |
| RANGE | 1,950 miles (T–39A) |
| | over 2,100 miles (Srs 40) |
| | over 2,000 miles (Srs 60) |

## Production

*NA–246:* N4060K.
*T–39A:* 59–2868 to 59–2872, 60–3478 to 60–3508, 61–634 to 61–685, 62–4448 to 62–4502.
*T–39B:* 59–2873 to 59–2874, 60–3474 to 60–3477.
*T–39D:* 150542 to 155051, 150969 to 150992, 151336 to 151343.
*VT–39E:* 157352 to 157354, plus later contracts.
Commercial aircraft deliveries not listed.

Top right: *The prototype Sabreliner 60 (NA–306).*

Right: *The prototype Sabre 75, with square windows and deepened fuselage.*

# OV–10 Bronco

In August 1964, North American's Columbus Division was named the winner of a tri-service design competition for a new category of light armed reconnaissance aircraft. The competition had been launched late in 1963 after several years of study by the US Marine Corps of the counter-insurgency type aeroplanes that were intended to fit in the operational spectrum between armed helicopters and heavier tactical aircraft. The USAF and US Army joined in writing a specification for this aeroplane, and North American was one of eleven companies submitting designs to meet the requirement.

The NA–300 design was a twin-boom, high wing aeroplane with pilot and observer seated in tandem beneath a large canopy for maximum view all round, and additional space for freight, stretchers or paratroops in the square-section fuselage pod. Emphasis was placed upon simple and straight-forward construction for minimum cost, and ease of maintenance for high utilisation in combat conditions. Power was supplied by two Garrett AiResearch T76 turbo-props, and built in armament of four 7·62mm machine guns could be supplemented by bombs, rockets, mini-gun pods, long-range tanks, etc, on seven external strong points.

Top right: *Second prototype YOV–10A (NA–300) with original short wing and straight sponsons.*

Right: *Modified YOV–10A prototype with Hoerner wing tips and angled sponsons.*

The initial contract was for seven prototypes designated YOV–10A, and the first flight was made at Columbus on July 16th, 1965. The seventh and last YOV–10A was fitted with Pratt & Whitney T74 (PT6A) engines for comparative purposes and first flew on October 7th, 1966. As originally built, the prototype had a span of 30ft, with completely squared-off wing tips; 660hp T76–G–6/8 engines and gross weight of 10,550lb. To meet the performance guarantees with greatly increased equipment loads subsequently specified, the production standard OV–10A was modified to have a 40ft span wing with faired Hoerner-type tips, the booms moved outwards six inches, 715hp T76–G–10/12 engines and maximum gross weight of 14,444lb. A YOV–10A modified to this standard flew for the first time in March 1967.

Production of the OV–10A, named Bronco, was authorised in October 1966, by which time specific requirements had been raised by the Marine Corps and the Air Force. Both needed the type for operations in Vietnam, primarily in the Forward Air Controller rôle. This activity involved visual spotting of enemy targets and directing tactical strike aircraft to their targets. The ability of the Bronco to carry a substantial weapon load allowed FACs to attack targets of opportunity themselves,

Top right: *US Marine Corps OV–10A carrying rocket pods for Vietnam strike.*

Right: *USAF OV–10A operating as Forward Air Controller over Vietnam.*

often making it unnecessary to call in heavier aircraft.

Operations in Vietnam began with the Marine Corps on July 6th, 1968, using the first six aircraft attached to Squadron VMO–2. Subsequently, VMO–6 was also equipped with the Bronco in Vietnam, and the US Navy borrowed 18 OV–10As from the USMC to equip VA(L)–4 in a similar rôle. In the US, Marine Squadrons VMO–1, VMO–4 and VMO–8 also operated the Bronco, as well as the Navy training unit VS–41. USAF operations in Vietnam began a little after the Marine Corps, and the 19th, 20th and 23rd Tactical Air Support Squadrons were equipped. The USMC acquired 114 OV–10As in all, and the USAF, 157.

Two YOV–10Ds were procured for USMC testing in 1971, by modifying OV–10As. The changes comprised installation of a three-barrel 20mm cannon in a remotely-operated ventral turret, and a forward-looking infra-red sensor in the nose. These aircraft were known as Night Observation/Gunship Systems. An aerodynamic test vehicle modified from the second YOV–10A was first flown in the YOV–10D configuration on June 9th, 1970. In the USAF Pave Nail programme, thirteen OV–10As were converted for night forward air control and strike designation duties, with laser-rangefinder, target illu-

Top right: *An OV10B (Z) target tug with boost engine.*

Right: *One of the YOV–10D Night Observation Gunship System prototypes.*

minator and stabilised night periscope sight.

Production of the OV–10A for the USAF ended in April 1969, but North American subsequently received orders for thirty-two similar OV–10Cs for Thailand, sixteen OV–10Es for Venezuala and eighteen OV–10Bs for Germany. The latter were intended for use as target tugs, and twelve were modified as OV–10B (Z)s, each with a 2,950lb st J85–GE–4 turbojet above the fuselage, boosting the top speed from 241 knots to 341 knots. The first OV–10B(Z) was converted by North American, flying for the first time on September 3rd, 1970, the other 11 being converted by Rhein Flugzeugbau after delivery as OV–10Bs during 1971.

## Specification (OV–10A)

| | |
|---|---|
| SPAN | 40ft |
| LENGTH | 39ft 9in |
| HEIGHT | 15ft 1in |
| WING AREA | 291sq ft |
| GROSS WEIGHT | 14,444lb |
| MAX SPEED | 281mph at 10,000ft |
| LOITER SPEED | 127mph at 5,000ft |
| RANGE | 500 miles (typical mission) |

### Production
YOV–10A: 152879/152885.
OV–10A: 155390/155503, 66–13552/13562, 67–14604/14701, 68–3784/3831.
OV–10B: D–9545/9562.
OV–10C: 1/2513–4/2513, 5/2514–16/2514 (plus second batch of 16).

*A 1970-model Shrike Commander-Esquire.*

# Shrike Commander

The Aero Commander name originated in 1950 when Aero Design and Engineering Corporation was set up to produce an aircraft known as the Aero Commander L.3805, a six-seven seat light twin-engined monoplane based on an earlier prototype known as the Baumann Brigadier. The L.3805 was the progenitor of a long line of Aero Commanders, including several models retained in production by North American–Rockwell after acquisition of Aero Commander.

The basic piston-engined Aero Commander acquired was the Model 500–U, which had been certificated on December 11th, 1954, with two 290hp Lycoming IO–540–E1A5 or E1B5 engines. With the characteristic Aero Commander high wing, single tail, layout, the 500–U seated four in its standard form or up to eight with alternative layouts. It was named the Shrike Commander when names were given to all the Aero Commander range, and with refinements remained in production by NR at the time this volume was prepared. A more luxuriously-appointed variant aimed at the business owner/pilot was named the Shrike Esquire.

## Specification

| | |
|---|---|
| SPAN | 49ft 0½in |
| LENGTH | 36ft 7in |
| HEIGHT | 14ft 6in |
| WING AREA | 255sq ft |
| GROSS WEIGHT | 6,750lb |
| MAX SPEED | 215mph |
| CRUISING SPEED | 203mph |
| RANGE | 750 miles |

## Courser Commander, Commander 685

On December 29th, 1962, Aero Commander flew the prototype of a new model which it called the Grand Commander, with a longer fuselage than the variants already in production. Certificated on May 24th, 1963, as the Model 680FL, it was powered by two Lycoming IGSO–540–B1A or –B1C engines and seated 5–7 passengers in the cabin plus the two pilots.

This model was later named the Courser Commander and a version equipped to carry nine passengers was marketed as the Courser Liner, but the type was sold only in small numbers and was dropped from the NR range of business aircraft at the end of 1969. During 1971, certification was obtained for the Aero Commander 685, based on the pressurised Turbo-Commander airframe but powered by two 435hp Continental GTSIO–520–F engines. This 7–9-seater had a gross weight of 9,000lb.

### Specification

| | |
|---|---|
| SPAN | 49ft 2½in |
| LENGTH | 41ft 6in |
| HEIGHT | 14ft 6in |
| WING AREA | 255sq ft |
| GROSS WEIGHT | 8,500lb |
| CRUISING SPEED | 225mph |
| RANGE | 1,160 miles |

*The Courser Commander.*

# Turbo Commander, Hawk Commander

Aero Commander flew its first turboprop variant on December 31st, 1964, as the Turbo Commander, powered by two 575shp AiResearch TPE-331 engines. After some development problems had been overcome, this pressurised variant was certificated as the Model 680T on September 15th, 1965, with uprated 605shp TPE-331-43 turbo-props, and was marketed as the Turbo II Commander, deliveries starting in May 1966. An improved model, with gross weight increased from 8,950lb to 9,400lb, was certificated in June 1967 as Model 680V and TPE-331-43BL engines were introduced in the Model 680W the following year.

Further small improvements were represented by the Model 681, certificated on March 20th, 1969, and in the same year the name Turbo II Commander was dropped in favour of Hawk Commander, which was offered with standard seating for eight including the two pilots. The name was abandoned in 1971, however, when the Hawk Commander was succeeded by the Turbo Commander 681B, with minor changes including a slightly lengthened nose, and a much-reduced selling price. This model was dropped from the NR range in 1972.

Top right: *A 1970-model Hawk Commander.*

Right: *This Hawk Commander was converted by Turboméca in 1971 as a test-bed for Astafan turbofan engines.*

*The Turbo Commander 690.*

# Quail Commander, Sparrow Commander, Snipe Commander

These two agricultural aeroplanes originated in 1956 with a product of the Call Aircraft Co, known as the CallAir A–4 Ag. The design was later acquired by Intermountain Manufacturing Co (IMCO), which evolved from it the A–9. The latter was in turn acquired by Aero Commander and put into production as the Ag Commander A–9, being given the name Quail Commander in 1968 after the NAA–Rockwell merger.

The Quail Commander was typical of ag–planes in its general layout, with design emphasis on simplicity, manoeuvrability, good pilot visibility, resistance to corrosion from insecticide, good load-carrying and so on. Power was supplied by a 290hp Lycoming IO–540–G1C5 engine and a version with a 235hp Lycoming O–540–B2B5 engine was later added to the range as the A–9A Sparrow Commander.

Replacing the Hawk Commander in the higher-price bracket, the Turbo Commander 690 was first flown on March 3rd, 1969, being certificated on July 19th, 1971, with 700shp TPE–331–5–251K turboprops. Although outwardly similar to the Hawk Commander in appearance, the 690 was a considerable modification aimed at improving performance and reducing cabin noise levels. This was achieved by using a geared engine to slow down propeller speed and moving the engines 15in outboard on a new wider-span centre section. Propeller diameter was increased and the fin and rudder area increased.

### Specification

|  | 681B | 690 |
| --- | --- | --- |
| SPAN | 44ft 0¾in | 46ft 6in |
| LENGTH | 42ft 11¾in | 42ft 11¾in |
| HEIGHT | 14ft 6in | — |
| WING AREA | 242·5sq ft | 266sq ft |
| GROSS WEIGHT | 9,450lb | 10,250lb |
| MAX SPEED | 290mph | 327mph |
| CRUISING SPEED | 278mph | 316mph |
| RANGE | 1,315 miles | 1,469 miles |

Production of both these types—totalling over 300—continued at the Albany works until 1971, when NR sold the design rights, tooling and production materials to Aeronautica Agricola Mexicana SA in Mexico. The latter company, in which NR had a thirty per cent interest, began production of the two types in 1972.

In addition to the IMCO A–9, Aero Commander acquired from Intermountain Manufacturing Co the design of a similar but larger agricultural aeroplane known as the B–1. The prototype was powered by a 400hp Lycoming IO–720–A1A engine but Aero Commander substituted the 450hp Pratt & Whitney IR–985–AN3 radial in a production version known as the B–1A Snipe Commander. Only nine were delivered by NR before this model was dropped from the company's agricultural range.

### Specification

|  | Quail | Sparrow |
|---|---|---|
| SPAN | 34ft 9in | 34ft 9in |
| LENGTH | 23ft 6in | 23ft 6in |
| HEIGHT | 7ft 7in | 7ft 7in |
| WING AREA | 182sq ft | 182sq ft |
| GROSS WEIGHT | 3,600lb | 3,400lb |
| MAX SPEED | 120mph | 119mph |
| CRUISING SPEED | 100mph | 95mph |
| RANGE | 275 miles | 250 miles |

Left: *The Quail Commander ag-plane, originally a CallAir design.*

Top right: *A Sparrow Commander in action.*

Right: *The Snipe Commander.*

# Thrush Commander

Like the Quail Commander, the Thrush Commander came into the NR range by way of the Aero Commander Division of Rockwell, which had in turn acquired the design in 1965 from Snow Aeronautical Corp. As the Snow S-2, the type had been in production since 1958. It was produced by Aero Commander as the Ag Commander and then extensively redesigned and updated by NR in 1968 as the Thrush Commander.

Powered by a 600hp Pratt & Whitney R-1340-AN1 radial, the Thrush Commander had a 53cu ft hopper with a capacity of 400 US gallons, giving it one of the largest capacities of any American agricultural monoplane. By 1972, it was also the only agricultural aircraft retained in the NR range, remaining in production at Albany. Over 250 had been built by the end of 1971.

## Specification

| | |
|---|---|
| SPAN | 44ft 5in |
| LENGTH | 29ft 4½in |
| HEIGHT | 9ft 2in |
| WING AREA | 326·6sq ft |
| GROSS WEIGHT | 6,900lb |
| MAX SPEED | 140mph |
| CRUISING SPEED | 124mph |
| RANGE | 403 miles |

Top left: *The Thrush Commander, derived from the Snow S-2.*

Left: *The 1968-model Darter Commander.*

# Darter Commander, Lark Commander

During 1965, Aero Commander added to its range of light aircraft by acquiring Volaircraft Inc, a small organisation then in production with the Volaire Model 10 and Model 10A high-wing lightplane with, respectively, three and four seats. At the time of the deal, Volaire had built only three Model 10s with 135hp Lycoming O–290–D2C engines and Aero Commander built another thirteen as their Model 100A. Shortly before the design was acquired by Aero Commander, the Model 10A was introduced with a 150hp Lycoming O–320–A2B engine and six were built by the original company. Aero Commander continued production as the Model 100 and this type was later named Darter Commander, remaining in production until 1969 as an NR product, by which time nearly 200 had been built.

During 1967, a refined version was introduced as the Model 100–180 Lark Commander powered by a 180hp Lycoming O–360–A2F flat four engine. This model had a redesigned swept-back fin, improved streamlining of the cowling, wheel fairings etc, and other detail refinements. More than 200 had been built by the end of 1971, when design rights in both the Darter and Lark Commander were sold by NR to Phoenix Aircraft.

## Specification

|  | Darter | Lark |
| --- | --- | --- |
| SPAN | 35ft | 35ft |
| LENGTH | 22ft 6in | 27ft 2in |
| HEIGHT | 9ft 4in | 10ft 1in |
| WING AREA | 181sq ft | 180sq ft |
| GROSS WEIGHT | 2,250lb | 2,475lb |
| MAX SPEED | 133mph | 138mph |
| CRUISING SPEED | 128mph | 132mph |
| RANGE | 510 miles | 560 miles |

*The Lark Commander, with distinguishing back-swept fin.*

## Aero Commander Models 111 and 112

The first original design produced by the NR General Aviation Division following the merging of Aero Commander with North American was an attractive four-seat low-wing monoplane known as the Model 112. Design of a new series of light-planes in this category was started late in 1969 and the first of five prototypes of the Model 112 made its first flight on December 4th, 1970, powered by a 180hp Lycoming O–360–A1G6 engine.

On September 11th, 1971, flight testing of the Model 111 began. Similarly powered, this differed primarily in having a fixed undercarriage. Certification was delayed by a few months by the need to introduce modifications to overcome a problem with the tail unit design, and deliveries began in the second half of 1972. In production form, the Model 112 had a 200hp engine and the Model 111A had a constant-speed propeller.

### Specification

|  | 111 | 112 |
| --- | --- | --- |
| SPAN | 32ft 10¾in | 32ft 10¾in |
| LENGTH | 25ft 0in | 25ft 0in |
| HEIGHT | 8ft 5in | 8ft 5in |
| WING AREA | 152sq ft | 152sq ft |
| GROSS WEIGHT | 2,500lb | 2,550lb |
| MAX SPEED | 150mph | 170mph |
| CRUISING SPEED | 142mph | 162mph |
| RANGE | 1,010 miles | 1,180 miles |
|  | (no reserves) | |

*Prototypes of the Aero Commander Models 111 (nearest camera) and 112.*

## B–1

To take the place of the cancelled B–70 in USAF advanced planning, proposals were drawn up in 1965 for an Advanced Manned Strategic Aircraft (AMSA) and changing political and defence environments made it possible for a specific requirement for this supersonic bomber to be drawn up in 1969. In November of that year, requests for proposals were issued to industry, and North American Rockwell and Boeing were subsequently chosen to undertake feasibility studies. Selection of the submission made by NR was announced by the USAF early in June 1970, the aircraft being designated B–1A as a supersonic strategic bomber.

The operational requirement was for an aircraft with an unrefuelled range of over 6,000 miles, a maximum speed of Mach 2.2, a Mach 0·85 cruising speed and the ability to fly a terrain-following profile at very high subsonic speed in order to approach its target 'under the radar'. Primary armament was to comprise Boeing SRAMs (short-range attack missiles) launched some distance from the target, with provision for nuclear or conventional bombs.

To meet the requirement, NR chose a variable geometry design, the wing panels being hinged to sweep back outboard of nacelles each housing a pair of 30,000lb st General Electric F101–GE–100 turbofan engines behind variable-area intakes. An area-ruled fuselage and blended wing-fuselage contours excluding all sharp lines contributed to the B–1A's high aerodynamic and structural efficiency. A four-man crew was located in a capsule that could be ejected intact for emergency escape, and the

*An artist's impression of the North American Rockwell B–1A.*

fuselage contained three weapon bays with rotary launchers.

The original contract provided for construction of two test specimens and five flying prototypes and production of up to 240 B–1s was envisaged to meet SAC requirements. As an economy measure, the programme was subsequently reduced to three flying prototypes and full development of the avionics system and other related equipment was delayed until after flight testing, scheduled to begin in April 1974. Production aircraft, if the programme was given the go-ahead in April 1975, were to fly in 1976, with deliveries to SAC starting in October 1977.

**Specification**

| | |
|---|---|
| SPAN | 136ft 8in (forward) |
| | 78ft 2½in (swept) |
| LENGTH | 143ft 4in |
| HEIGHT | 33ft 7in |
| GROSS WEIGHT | 380,000lb (about) |
| MAX SPEED | Mach 2·2 |
| RANGE | 6,000 miles (over) |

## Type and Production List

The following list provides information on North American Charge Numbers allocated from the beginning of 1935 to 1967 and a few more recent numbers available for publication. The 'originating date' is the date given in company records and is not necessarily the date on which a contract was actually placed with the company. In the 'Customer' column, parentheses indicate the final customer for aircraft built originally as private ventures. Parentheses in the 'Quantity built' column indicate converted aircraft.

The abbreviations in the 'Works' column are: MD—Dundalk, Maryland; I—Inglewood (Los Angeles); T—Dallas, Texas; K—Kansas City; LB—Long Beach; D—Downey; LA—Los Angeles; C—Columbus; F—Fresno. Abbreviations in the 'Customer' column are: USAAC—US Army Air Corps; USAAF—US Army Air Force; USAF—US Air Force; USN—US Navy; NG—National Guard; CAC—Commonwealth Aircraft Company; RAF—Royal Air Force; RCAF—Royal Canadian Air Force.

## Postscript

Early in 1973, as these pages went to press, the North American Rockwell Corporation changed its name to Rockwell International. As a result, the business, private and agricultural aircraft types then in production became identified simply as 'Rockwell' rather than 'North American' products. Only the military aircraft built at Los Angeles and Columbus continued to be identified as 'North American' types.

| CHARGE NUMBER | ORIGINATING DATE | NAME OR DESIGNATION | CUSTOMER | WORKS | DESCRIPTION | QNTY BUILT | CONSTRUCTOR'S NUMBERS |
|---|---|---|---|---|---|---|---|
| GA–15 | — | XO–47 | USAAC | MD | Observation monoplane | 1 | GA–15–1 |
| NA–16 | — | NA–16 | Company | MD | Basic trainer demonstrator, open cockpit | 1 | NA–16–1 |
| NA–17 | — | — | USN | MD | Sets of one main and two wing floats for Curtiss SOC–1 | 161 | — |
| NA–18 | 13·5·35 | NA–16 | (Argentina) | I | NA–16 modified, enclosed cockpits | (1) | NA–16–1 |
| NA–19 | 3·10·35 | BT–9 | USAAC | I | Production basic trainer based on NA–16 | 42 | NA–19–1, –3, –5 to –11, –20 to –34, –50 to –67 |
| NA–19A | — | BT–9A | USAAC | I | As BT–9 for Army Air Corps Reserve | 40 | NA–19–4, –12 to –19, –35 to –49, –68 to –83 |
| NA–20 | — | NA–16–2H | (Honduras) | I | Demonstrator | 1 | NA–16–2 |
| NA–21 | — | XB–21 | USAAC | I | Medium bomber | 1 | NA–21–84 |
| NA–22 | — | NA–22 | Company | I | BT–9 (36–36) modified with open cockpits | (1) | — |
| NA–23 | 1·12·36 | BT–9B | USAAC | I | Improved NA–19 | 117 | NA–23–85 to –201 |
| NA–24 | — | — | USN | — | Sets of one main and two wing floats for Curtiss SOC–1 | 48 | 24–323 to –418 (wing); 24–1078 to –1125 |
| NA–25 | — | O–47A | USAAC NG | I I | Production of GA–15 Production of GA–15 | 71 93 | 25–203 to –266, –541 to –547 25–267 to –311, –548 to –595 |
| NA–26 | 20·10·36 | NA–26 | (RCAF) | I | First NA–16 type with retractable u/c | 1 | 26–202 |
| NA–27 | 1·12·36 | NA–16–2H | Fokker | I | As NA–26 for European demonstration | 1 | 27–312 |
| NA–28 | 14·12·36 | NJ–1 | USN | I | Navy variant of BT–9 | 40 | 28–313 to –352 |
| NA–29 | 22·12·36 | BT–9C | USAAC | I | As BT–9B with armament; 29–385 delivered as Y1BT–10 | 67 | 29–353 to –385, –505 to –538 |
| NA–30 | — | Y1BT–10 | — | I | Drawings only | | |
| NA–31 | 8·2·37 | NA–16–4M | Flygvapnet | I | Pattern aircraft similar to BT–9, sold with production licence | 1 | 31–386 |
| NA–32 | 10·3·37 | NA–16–1A | CAC | I | Pattern aircraft similar to NA–26 with fixed u/c | 1 | 32–387 |
| NA–33 | 10·3·37 | NA–16–2K | CAC | I | As NA–32 with retractable gear, sold with production licence | 1 | 33–388 |
| NA–34 | 19·3·37 | NA–16–4P | Argentina | I | As BT–9 with added armament | 30 | 34–389 to –418 |
| NA–35 | — | NA–35 | Company | I | Civil or military light open two-seater | 1 | 35–419 |
| NA–36 | 13·6·37 | BC–1 | USAAC | I | Production version of NA–26 | 177 | 36–420 to –504, –596 to –687 |
| NA–37 | 2·9·37 | NA–16–4R | Japan | I | Pattern aircraft similar to BT–9, sold with production licence | 1 | 37–539 |
| NA–38 | 28·9·37 | NA–16–4M | Flygvapnet | I | As NA–31, but shipped disassembled | 1 | 38–540 |
| NA–39 | — | XB–21 | USAAC | I | Modifications to NA–21 | (1) | 21–84 |
| NA–40 | — | NA–40 | Company | I | Twin-engined attack bomber demonstrator | 1 | 40–1052 |
| NA–41 | 23·2·38 | NA–16–4 | China | I | Similar to BT–9C | 35 | 41–697 to –731 |
| NA–42 | 9·12·37 | NA–16–2A | Honduras | I | Similar to NA–20 with armament | 2 | 42–691 and –692 |
| NA–43 | 9·12·37 | NA–16–1G | — | I | BT–9C variant design for Brazilian Army Air Force | — | — |
| NA–44 | 9·12·37 | NA–44 | (RCAF) | I | Light attack bomber demonstrator | 1 | 44–747 |
| NA–45 | 14·12·37 | NA–16–1GV | Venezuela | I | Similar to BC–1 | 3 | 45–693 to –695 |
| NA–46 | 2·12·38 | NA–16–4 | Brazil | I | BT–9C variant for Brazilian Navy | 12 | 46–972 to –977, –1991 to –1996 |
| NA–47 | 16·12·37 | NA–16–4RW | Japan | I | Similar to NA–37 with different engine. Shipped disassembled | 1 | 47–696 |
| NA–48 | 23·2·38 | NA–16–3C | China | I | Similar to BC–1 with different engine | 15 | 48–732 to –746 |

| CHARGE NUMBER | ORIGINATING DATE | NAME OR DESIGNATION | CUSTOMER | WORKS | DESCRIPTION | QNTY BUILT | CONSTRUCTOR'S NUMBERS |
|---|---|---|---|---|---|---|---|
| NA-49 | 7·2·38 | NA-16-1E Harvard I | RAF | I | As NA-36 with improvements and British equipment | 400 | 49-748 to -947, -1053 to -1252 |
| NA-50 | — | NA-50 | Peru | I | Single-seat fighter based on NA-26 design | 7 | 50-948 to -954 |
| NA-51 | — | O-47B | USAAC | I | Variant of NA-25 | 74 | 51-978 to -1051 |
| NA-52 | 28·9·38 | SNJ-1 | USN | I | Similar to BC-1 with some NA-44 features | 16 | 52-956 to -971 |
| NA-53 | — | — | — | I | Single-seat fighter design, cancelled | — | |
| NA-54 | 3·10·38 | BC-2 | USAAC | I | As BC-1 with improvements of NA-44 | 3 | 54-688 to -690 |
| NA-55 | | BC-1A | USAAC | I | As BC-2 with ungeared engine | 83 | 55-1548 to -1630 |
| NA-56 | 18·4·39 | NA-16-4 | China | I | Similar to NA-55 with fixed gear | 50 | 56-1453 to -1502 |
| NA-57 | 21·2·39 | NA-57 | France | I | Improved version of NA-23 | 230 | 57-1253 to -1452, -1518 to -1547 |
| NA-58 | 28·4·39 | BT-14 | USAAC | I | Similar to BT-9B with some BC-1A features | 251 | 58-1655 to -1905 |
| NA-59 | 28·4·39 | AT-6 | USAAC | I | Same as BC-1A, with designation change | 94 | 59-1631 to -1639, -1906 to -1990 |
| NA-60 | — | O-47A | USAAC | I | Re-work of final NA-25 | (1) | 25-595 |
| NA-61 | 25·5·39 | NA-16-1E Harvard I | RCAF | I | Almost identical with NA-49 | 30 | 61-1503 to -1517, -1640 to -1654 |
| NA-62 | — | B-25, -25A, -25B | USAAC | I | Medium bomber developed from NA-40 | 184 | 62-2834 to -3017 |
| NA-63 | — | XB-28 | USAAC | I | Twin-engined high-altitude bomber | 1 | 63-2233 |
| NA-64 | — | NA-64 (Yale I) | France | I | Similar to NA-57 with improvements. Last 119 became Yale | 230 | 64-2033 to -2232, -3018 to -3047 |
| NA-65 | 25·9·39 | SNJ-2 | USN | I | As SNJ-1 with new features of BC-1A | 36 | 65-1997 to -2032 |
| NA-66 | 17·11·39 | Harvard II | RAF | I | Similar to AT-6. Two crashed before delivery | 600 | 66-2234 to -2833 |
| NA-67 | — | XB-28A | USAAC | I | Similar to XB-28. Crashed on test flight | 1 | 67-3417 |
| NA-68 | — | NA-50A | Siam | I | Similar to NA-50. Diverted to USAAC as P-64 | 6 | 68-3058 to -3063 |
| NA-69 | — | NA-44 | Siam | I | Similar to NA-44. Diverted to USAAC as A-27 | 10 | 69-3064 to -3073 |
| NA-70 | — | — | — | I | NA-35 two-seat primary trainer, cancelled | — | — |
| NA-71 | 18·1·40 | NA-16-3 | Venezuela | I | Similar to NA-59 | 3 | 71-3074 to -3076 |
| NA-72 | 13·1·40 | NA-44 | Brazil | I | Attack bomber based on NA-44 demonstrator | 30 | 72-3077 to -3096, -4757 to -4766 |
| NA-73X | — | NA-73X | Company | I | Prototype single-seat fighter with laminar wing | 1 | 73-3097 |
| NA-73 | — | Mustang I | RAF | I | Production form of NA-73X | 320 | 73-3098 to -3100, -3102 to -3106, -3108 to -3416, -4767 to -4768, -7812 |
| NA-73 | — | XP-51 | USAAC | I | Evaluation models of Mustang I | 2 | 73-3101, 73-3107 |
| NA-74 | 7·8·40 | NA-44 | Chile | I | Same as NA-72 | 12 | 74-4745 to -4756 |
| NA-75 | 3·6·40 | Harvard II | RCAF | I | Same as NA-66 | 100 | 75-3048 to -3057, -3418 to -3507 |
| NA-76 | 5·6·40 | Harvard II | RAF | I | Same as NA-66; French order taken over by Britain | 450 | 76-3508 to -3957 |
| NA-77 | 28·6·40 | AT-6A | USAAC | I | Similar to NA-66 | 517 | 77-3958 to -3982 |
| | | SNJ-3 | USN | I | Navy version of AT-6A | 120 | 77-4133 to -4744 |
| NA-78 | 1·10·40 | AT-6A/SNJ-3 | USAAC/USN | T | As NA-77 built at Dallas, Texas | 1,480 | — |
| NA-79 | 24·6·40 | SNJ-2 | USN | I | Similar to NA-65 | 25 | 78-3983 to -4007 |
| NA-80 | — | — | — | — | Cancelled project | — | — |

| CHARGE NUMBER | ORIGINATING DATE | NAME OR DESIGNATION | CUSTOMER | WORKS | DESCRIPTION | QNTY BUILT | CONSTRUCTOR'S NUMBERS |
|---|---|---|---|---|---|---|---|
| NA–81 | 11·7·40 | Harvard II | RAF | I | Same as NA–66 | 125 | 81–4008 to 81–4132 |
| NA–82 | — | B–25C | USAAC | I | Improved version of NA–62 | 863 | 82–5069 to 82–5931 |
| NA–83 | — | Mustang I | RAF | I | Improved version of NA–73 | 300 | 83–4769 to –5068 |
| NA–84 | 6·12·40 | AT–6B | USAAC | T | Improved version of NA–77 | 400 | 78–7412 to –7811 |
| NA–85 | — |  | USN | T | SNJ–3 contract transferred to NA–78 | — | — |
| NA–86 | — | — | — | — | Cancelled project | — | — |
| NA–87 | — | B–25D | USAAF | K | As NA–82, built at Kansas City plant | 1,200 | 87–7813 to –9012 |
| NA–88 | 10·4·41 | AT–6C/D, SNJ–4/5 | USAAF/USN | T | Improved version of NA–84 | 9,331 |  |
| NA–89 | — |  | — | — | Proposed production of NA–63, cancelled | — | — |
| NA–90 | — | B–25C | Netherlands | I | Contract for Netherlands, taken over by USAAF | 162 | 90–11819 to –11980 |
| NA–91 | — | Mustang IA | USAAF | I | Defence Aid contract for RAF; some retained by USAAF | 150 | 91–11981 to –12130 |
| NA–92 | — | — | — | — | Boeing B–29 contract, cancelled |  |  |
| NA–93 | — | B–25C | USAAF | I | Defence Aid contract for China | 150 | 93–12491 to –12640 |
| NA–94 | — | B–25C | USAAF | I | Defence Aid contract for RAF | 150 | 94–12641 to –12790 |
| NA–95 | — | B–24G | USAAF | T | Production of Convair Liberator; 434 more cancelled | 966 | 95–15131 to –15880, –36536 to –36751 |
| NA–96 | — | B–25C | USAAF | I | Continuation of NA–82 | 300 | 96–16381 to –16680 |
|  |  | B–25G |  |  | As B–25C with 75mm cannon | 400 | 96–16681 to –16780, –20806 to –21105 |
| NA–97 | — | A–36 | USAAF | I | Dive bomber derived from NA–73 | 500 | 97–15881 to –16380 |
| NA–98 | — | B–25H | USAAF | I | Improved development of NA–96 | 1,000 | 98–21106 to –22105 |
| NA–99 | — | P–51A | USAAF | I | As NA–73 with armament change | 310 | 99–22106 to –22415 |
| NA–100 | — | B–25D | USAAF | K | Continuation of NA–87 | 1,090 | 100–20606 to –20805, –23306 to –24195 |
| NA–101 | — | XP–51B | USAAF | I | Two NA–91s with Merlin engine installation | (2) | 91–12013 and –12082 |
| NA–102 | — | P–51B | USAAF | I | As NA–101 with Packard-built Merlin | 400 | 102–24541 to –24940 |
| NA–103 | — | P–51C | USAAF | T | As NA–102 built at Dallas | 1,350 | 103–22416 to –22815, –25933 to –26882 |
| NA–104 | — | P–51B | USAAF | I | Improved version of NA–102 | 1,588 | 104–22816 to –23305, –24431 to –24540, –24941 to –25340, –25343 to –25930 |
| NA–105 | — | XP–51F | USAAF | I | Lightweight P–51 with V–1650–3 engine | 3 | 105–26883 to –26885 |
|  |  | XP–51G | USAAF | I | Lightweight P–51 with Merlin RM–14SM engine | 2 | 105–25931 to –25932 |
|  |  | XP–51J | USAAF | I | Lightweight P–51 with Allison V–1710–119 engine | 2 | 105–47446 to –47447 |
| NA–106 | — | P–51D | USAAF | I | P–51 with new canopy and increased armament | 2 | 106–25341 to –25342 |
| NA–107 | — | — | — | — | Contract for 950 P–51C transferred to NA–103 |  | — |
| NA–108 | — | B–25J | USAAF | K | Similar to NA–98 with bombardier nose. Includes 72 built but not delivered; 415 more on order cancelled | 4,390 | 108–24196 to –24430, –31986 to 35535, –37186 to –37585, –47446 to –47750 |
| NA–109 | — | P–51D | USAAF | I | Same as NA–106 | 2,500 | 109–26886 to –28885, –35536 to –36035 |
| NA–110 | — | P–51D | USAAF | I | As NA–109, shipped unassembled to Australia | 100 | 110–34386 to –34485 |

| CHARGE NUMBER | ORIGINATING DATE | NAME OR DESIGNATION | CUSTOMER | WORKS | DESCRIPTION | QNTY BUILT | CONSTRUCTOR'S NUMBERS |
|---|---|---|---|---|---|---|---|
| NA–111 | — | P–51C | USAAF | T | Same as NA–103 | 400 | 111–28886 to –29285 |
| | | P–51D | USAAF | T | Same as NA–109 | 600 | 111–29286 to –29485, –36136 to –36535 |
| | | P–51K | USAAF | T | As NA–109 with Aeroproducts propeller | 1,500 | 111–29486 to –30885, –36036 to –36135 |
| NA–112 | — | — | — | — | Contract for 2,000 P–51D transferred to NA–109 | — | — |
| NA–113 | — | — | — | — | Contract for B–25H, terminated | — | — |
| NA–114 | — | — | — | — | Contract for 1,050 B–25J transferred to NA–108 | — | — |
| NA–115 | — | — | — | — | Contract for 2,400 B–25J transferred to NA–108 | — | — |
| NA–116 | — | — | — | — | Experimental four-engined twin-boom heavy bomber, cancelled | — | — |
| NA–117 | — | — | — | — | Contract for 2,500 P–51H transferred to NA–126 | — | — |
| NA–118 | — | — | — | T | Contract for 650 B–24G transferred to NA–95 | — | |
| NA–119 | 10·1·44 | AT–6D | USAAF | T | Shipped to Brazil | 81 | 119–40086 to –40166 |
| NA–120 | — | XP–82 | USAAF | I | Prototype Twin Mustang fighter. Two more cancelled | 2 | 120–43742 to –43743 |
| NA–121 | 11·2·44 | AT–6D | USAAF | T | As NA–88 | 800 | 121–41567 to –42366 |
| | | AT–6F | | | Improved NA–88 | 956 | 121–42367 to –43322 |
| NA–122 | — | P–51D Mustang | USAAF | I | Same as NA–109 | 4,000 | 122–30886 to –31985, –38586 to –40085, –40167 to –41566 |
| NA–123 | — | P–82B/C/D | USAAF | I | Production version of NA–120. Contract cut from 500 | 20 | 123–43746 to –43765 |
| NA–124 | — | P–51D | USAAF | T | Same as NA–109. Contract cut from 2,000 | 1,000 | 124–44246 to –44845, –48096 to –48495 |
| | | P–51M | USAAF | T | As P–51D with V–1650–9A engine | 1 | 124–48496 |
| NA–125 | — | — | | T | Contract for 300 B–24G cancelled | — | |
| NA–126 | — | P–51H | USAAF | I | Production derivative of NA–105. Contract cut from 2,400 | 555 | 126–37586 to –38140 |
| NA–127 | — | — | — | — | Contract for 1,400 P–51D transferred to NA–126 | — | — |
| NA–128 | — | — | — | T | Contract for 1,200 AT–6D, cancelled | — | — |
| NA–129 | — | — | — | — | Cancelled Army project | — | — |
| NA–130 | — | XB–45 | USAF | I | Four-jet bomber prototypes | 3 | 130–59479 to –59481 |
| NA–131 | — | — | — | — | Cancelled Army project | — | — |
| NA–132 | — | — | — | — | Contract for B–29 tail units, cancelled | — | — |
| NA–133 | — | — | — | — | Cancelled Navy project | — | — |
| NA–134 | — | XFJ–1 Fury | USN | I | Carrier-based jet fighter | 3 | 134–55996 to –55998 |
| NA–135 | — | C–82N | USAF | T | Flying Box-car production; contract cut from 792 | 3 | 135–49496 to –49498 |
| NA–136 | — | — | — | — | Experimental aircraft for USAF, cancelled | — | — |
| NA–137 | — | — | — | K | Contract for 1,000 Lockheed P–80N, cancelled | — | — |
| NA–138 | — | — | — | T | Contract for 629 P–51D, cancelled | — | — |

| CHARGE NUMBER | ORIGINATING DATE | NAME OR DESIGNATION | CUSTOMER | WORKS | DESCRIPTION | QNTY BUILT | CONSTRUCTOR'S NUMBERS |
|---|---|---|---|---|---|---|---|
| NA–139 | — | — | — | I | Contract for 2,500 P–51H, cancelled | — | |
| NA–140 | — | XP–86 Sabre | USAF | I | Single-seat jet fighter | 3 | 140–38424 to –38426 |
| NA–141 | — | FJ–1 | USN | I | Production model of NA–134 | 30 | 141–38394 to –38423 |
| NA–142 | — | XSN2J–1 | USN | I | Scout-trainer prototypes | 2 | 142–38427 to –38428 |
| NA–143 | — | Navion | Company | I | Commercial lightplane prototypes | 2 | 143–1 and –2 |
| NA–144 | — | F–82E | USAF | I | Development of NA–123 | 100 | 144–38141 to –38240 |
| NA–145 | — | Navion | — | I | Production version of NA–143 | 1,027 | |
| NA–146 | — | XAJ–1 | USN | I | Carrier-based attack bomber prototypes | 3 | 146–38429 to –38431 |
| NA–147 | — | B–45A | USAF | I | Production model of NA–130. Last airframe for static test | 97 | 147–43401 to –43497 |
| NA–148 | 7·8·46 | — | — | | R & D project on commercial transport, cancelled | — | |
| NA–149 | 27·9·46 | F–82F | USAF | I | Night fighter, similar to NA–144 | 91 | 149–38291 to –38381 |
| NA–150 | 9·10·46 | F–82G | USAF | I | Night fighter, similar to NA–144 | 45 | 150–38241 to –38269 |
| | | F–82H | USAF | I | Winterised form of F–82G | 14 | 150–38382 to –38390 |
| NA–151 | 20·11·46 | F–86A | USAF | I | Production model of NA–140 | 221 | 151–38432 to –38464, –43498 to –43685 |
| NA–152 | 24·9·47 | — | — | I | Contract for 190 F–86B; 188 transferred to NA–151, 2 cancelled | — | |
| NA–153 | 17·10·47 | B–45C | USAF | LB | Similar to NA–147 with improvements | 10 | 153–38477 to –38486 |
| | | RB–45C | USAF | LB | As B–45C with cameras | 33 | 153–38487 to –38519 |
| NA–154 | 23·6·47 | L–17A | USAF | I | USAF purchase of NA–145 Navions from stock | 83 | — |
| NA–155 | 2·7·47 | — | USN | — | Mock-up of control and information centre (CIC) version of NA–146 | — | |
| NA–156 | 6·10·47 | AJ–1 | USN | D | Production model of NA–146 | 12 | 156–38465 to –38476 |
| NA–157 | 17·12·47 | YF–93A | USAF | I | Penetration fighter version of NA–151. Contract for 120; 118 cancelled | 2 | 157–1 and –2 |
| NA–158 | 8·4·48 | — | — | I | Engineering development of carrier attack bomber. See NA–163 | — | — |
| NA–159 | 6·5·48 | XT–28A | USAF | I | Prototypes and static test model of basic trainer | 3 | 159–1 to –3 |
| | | T–28A | USAF | I | Production basic trainer | 265 | 159–4 to –268 |
| NA–160 | 20·5·48 | AJ–1 | USN | D | Same as NA–156 | 28 | 160–1 to –28 |
| NA–161 | 11·6·48 | F–86A | USAF | LA | Similar to NA–151 | 333 | 161–1 to –333 |
| NA–162 | 17·6·48 | — | USAF | LB | Contract for 2 B–45C and 49 RB–45C, cancelled | — | |
| NA–163 | 1·10·48 | XA2J–1 | USN | LA | Carrier attack bomber developed from NA–156 | 2 | 163–1 and –2 |
| NA–164 | 28·3·49 | YF–86D | USAF | LA | Interceptor based on NA–161 with radar in nose | 2 | 164–1 and –2 |
| NA–165 | 4·4·49 | F–86D | USAF | LA | Production model of NA–164 | 153 | 165–1 to –153 |
| NA–166 | 5·5·49 | — | USAF | — | Contract for one all-weather version of F–93A, cancelled | — | |
| NA–167 | 16·8·49 | F–86J | USAF | LA | Installation of Avro Orenda in one F–86A | (1) | 161–63 |
| NA–168 | 5·10·49 | T–6G | USAF | D | Remanufacture of T–6 series | 691 | 168–1 to –691 |
| | | LT–6G | | | As T–6G, for use as 'spotters' in Korea | 59 | 168–692 to –750 |
| NA–169 | 30·9·49 | AJ–1 | USN | D | Continuation of NA–156 production | 15 | 169–1 to –15 |
| NA–170 | 15·11·49 | F–86E | USAF | LA | Improved NA–161 | 111 | 170–1 to –111 |

| CHARGE NUMBER | ORIGINATING DATE | NAME OR DESIGNATION | CUSTOMER | WORKS | DESCRIPTION | QNTY BUILT | CONSTRUCTOR'S NUMBERS |
|---|---|---|---|---|---|---|---|
| NA–171 | 9·2·50 | T–28A | USAF | D | As NA–159, built at Downey | 125 | 171–1 to –125 |
| NA–172 | 31·7·50 | F–86E | USAF | LA | Similar to NA–170 | 225 | 172–1 to –132, –268 to –360 |
| | | F–86F | USAF | LA | As F–86E with different engine provision | 135 | 172–133 to –267 |
| NA–173 | 1·8·50 | F–86D | USAF | LA | Same as NA–165 | 638 | 173–1 to –638 |
| NA–174 | 24·8·50 | T–28A | USAF | D | Similar to NA–171 with extra wing tanks | 744 | 174–1 to –744 |
| NA–175 | 18·8·50 | AJ–2P | USN | C | Reconnaissance version of NA–169 | 23 | 175–1 to –23 |
| NA–176 | 29·9·50 | F–86F | USAF | C | Similar to NA–172 | 441 | 176–1 to –441 |
| NA–177 | 15·12·50 | F–86D | USAF | LA | Same as NA–165 | 188 | 177–1 to –188 |
| NA–178 | 12·1·51 | — | USAF | — | Contract for 184 F–86E, cancelled | — | — |
| NA–179 | 15·1·51 | XFJ–2 | USN | LA | Navy version of NA–170 | 2 | 179–1 and –2 |
| NA–180 | 19·1·51 | YF–100A | USAF | LA | Prototypes of Super Sabre air superiority fighter | 2 | 180–1 and –2 |
| NA–181 | 30·1·51 | FJ–2 | USN | C | Production of NA–179 | 200 | 181–1 to –200 |
| NA–182 | 8·2·51 | T–6G | USAF | C | Remanufacture of T–6 series | 824 | 182–1 to –824 |
| NA–183 | 14·2·51 | AJ–2P | USN | C | Continuation of NA–175 production | 7 | 183–1 to –7 |
| NA–184 | 14·2·51 | AJ–2 | USN | C | As NA–156 with improvements of NA–175 | 55 | 184–1 to –55 |
| NA–185 | 19·3·51 | XFJ–2B | USN | LA | Variant of NA–181 with different armament | 1 | 185–1 |
| NA–186 | 22·6·51 | T–6J | USAF | C | Design data provided to CCF | — | |
| NA–187 | 16·3·51 | F–86H | USAF | LA | Fighter-bomber version of NA–172. Prototype and first production | 2 | 187–1 and –2 |
| | | | | C | As above | 173 | 187–3 to –175 |
| NA–188 | 11·4·51 | T–6G | USAF | LB | Remanufacture of T–6 series | 107 | 188–1 to –107 |
| NA–189 | 23·5·51 | T–28A | USAF | D | Similar to NA–174. Contract cut from 158 | 59 | 189–1 to –59 |
| NA–190 | 23·5·51 | F–86D | USAF | LA | Similar to NA–173 | 901 | 190–1 to –901 |
| NA–191 | 26·10·51 | F–86F | USAF | LA | Similar to NA–176 | 967 | 191–1 to –967 |
| NA–192 | 20·11·51 | F–100A | USAF | LA | Production model of NA–180 | 203 | 192–1 to –203 |
| NA–193 | 29·11·51 | F–86F Sabre | USAF | C | Same as NA–191, built at Columbus | 259 | 193–1 to –259 |
| NA–194 | 3·3·52 | FJ–3 Fury | USN | C | Similar to NA–181 | 389 | 194–1 to –389 |
| NA–195 | 19·3·52 | T–6G | USAF | F | Remanufacture of T–6 series | 11 | 195–1 to –11 |
| NA–196 | 2·5·52 | FJ–3 Fury | USN | C | Trial installation of J65–W–2 in FJ–2 airframe | (1) | |
| NA–197 | 16·6·52 | T–6G | USAF | F | Remanufacture of T–6D airframes | 110 | 197–1 to –50; 8002–1 to –60 |
| NA–198 | 3·7·52 | SNJ–8 | USN | — | Contract for 240 cancelled | | |
| NA–199 | 2·9·52 | T–28B | USN | D | Prototypes of USN version of T–28A | 2 | 199–1 and –2 |
| NA–200 | 27·8·52 | T–28B | USN | D | Production of NA–199 at Downey | 259 | 200–1 to –259 |
| | | | | C | Continuation of production at Columbus | 199 | 200–260 to –438 |
| NA–201 | 12·9·52 | F–86D | USAF | LA | As NA–190 with minor improvements | 624 | 201–1 to –624 |
| NA–202 | 12·9·52 | F–86F | USAF | LA | As NA–193 with 6–3 wing and improvements | 157 | 202–1 to –157 |
| NA–203 | 12·9·52 | F–86H | USAF | C | As NA–187 with 6–3 wing and improvements | 300 | 203–1 to –300 |
| NA–204 | 8·4·53 | TF–86F | Company | LA | F–86F Serial 52–5016 modified to 2-st trainer | (1) | 191–712 |
| NA–205 | 14·5·53 | YF–86K | USAF | LA | Modification of two F–86Ds for NATO programme | (2) | 190–33 and 190–207 |
| NA–206 | 14·5·53 | F–86F | USAF | LA | Contract for 240 aircraft, cancelled 13·8·53 | — | — |
| NA–207 | 18·6·53 | F–86K | USAF | LA | Fifty complete sets of airframe assemblies for NATO programme | 50 | — |
| NA–208 | 4·6·53 | FJ–4 | USN | C | Prototypes based on NA–194 | 2 | 208–1 and –2 |
| NA–209 | 4·6·53 | FJ–4 | USN | C | Production model of NA–208 | 150 | 209–1 to –150 |
| | | FJ–4B | USN | C | As above with additional armament | 71 | 209–151 to –221 |

| CHARGE NUMBER | ORIGINATING DATE | NAME OR DESIGNATION | CUSTOMER | WORKS | DESCRIPTION | QNTY BUILT | CONSTRUCTOR'S NUMBERS |
|---|---|---|---|---|---|---|---|
| NA–210 | 13·7·53 | F–86F | USAF | LA | Two F–86F modified to fire 1½-in rockets | (2) | 191–839 and 191–859 |
| NA–211 | 7·10·53 | F–100 | USAF | LA | Design and mock-up of F–100 interceptor | — | |
| NA–212 | 20·10·53 | F–107A | USAF | LA | Fighter-bomber prototypes; six others cancelled | 3 | 212–1 to –3 |
| NA–213 | 18·12·53 | F–86K | USAF | LA | As NA–207 but delivered fully assembled | 120 | 213–1 to –120 |
| NA–214 | 19·1·54 | F–100C | USAF | LA | Improved version of F–100A | 70 | 214–1 to –70 |
| NA–215 | 26·3·54 | FJ–3 | USN | C | Same as NA–194 | 149 | 215–1 to –149 |
| NA–216 | 23·3·54 | TF–86F | USAF | LA | F–86F Serial 53–1228 modified to 2-st trainer, as NA–204 | (1) | 216–1 |
| NA–217 | 26·3·54 | F–1000C | USAF | LA | Same as NA–214 | 381 | 217–1 to –381 |
| NA–218 | 11·6·54 | NA–218 | Japan | LA | One T–28B supplied to Mitsubishi Heavy Industries | 1 | 218–1 |
| NA–219 | 19·7·54 | T–28B | USN | C | Same as NA–200 | 51 | 219–1 to –51 |
| NA–220 | 26·7·54 | FJ–4 | USN | C | 45 FJ–4s, transferred to NA–209 contract | — | — |
| NA–221 | 3·8·54 | F–86K | USAF | LA | Seventy complete airframe sets, as NA–207 | 70 | — |
| NA–222 | 20·9·54 | F–100C | USAF | C | Same as NA–217 | 25 | 221–1 to –25 |
| NA–223 | 6·10·54 | F–100D | USAF | LA | Similar to NA–217 with improvements | 496 | 223–1 to –496 |
| NA–224 | 4·10·54 | F–100D | USAF | C | Same as NA–223, built at Columbus | 221 | 224–1 to –221 |
| NA–225 | 28·9·54 | T–28C | USN | C | Two T–28B, serials 138185 and 138187, modified | (2) | 200–256 and 200–258 |
| NA–226 | 21·10·54 | T–28C | USN | C | Production model of NA–225 | 243 | 226–1 to –243 |
| NA–227 | 28·10·54 | F–86F | USAF | LA | As NA–202 with improvements | 280 | 227–1 to –280 |
| NA–228 | 2·11·54 | FJ–3 | USN | C | 80 FJ–3, transferred to NA–215 contract | — | — |
| NA–229 | 2·11·54 | FJ–4 | USN | C | 46 FJ–4, transferred to NA–209 contract | — | — |
| NA–230 | 26·4·55 | TF–100C | USAF | LA | One F–100C, serial 54–1966, modified to 2-st trainer | (2) | 217–227 |
| NA–231 | 19·8·55 | F–86F | USAF | LA | Seventy complete airframe sets for Japan | 70 | — |
| NA–232 | 25·7·55 | F–86K | USAF | LA | Fifty-six sets of airframe assemblies, as NA–221 | 56 | — |
| NA–233 | 18·7·55 | A3J–1 | USN | C | Initial design and mock-up | — | — |
| NA–234 | 12·8·55 | FJ–4F | USN | C | Modification of two FJ–4s with monopropellant rocket engines | (2) | — |
| NA–235 | 23·9·55 | F–100D | USAF | LA | As NA–223 with provision for Sidewinder | 444 | 235–1 to –444 |
| NA–236 | 11·10·55 | LRI | USAF | LA | Engineering study of long-range interceptor | — | — |
| NA–237 | 6·12·55 | FBX | USAF | LA | Study of fighter-bomber system | — | — |
| NA–238 | 9·12·55 | F–86F | USAF | LA | 110 sets of airframe assemblies for Japan, as NA–231 | 110 | — |
| NA–239 | 9·12·55 | (XB–70) | USAF | LA | Engineering design and mock-up for Weapon System 110 | — | — |
| NA–240 | 9·12·55 | X–15 | USAF | LA | High altitude research aircraft | 3 | 240–1 to –3 |
| NA–241 | 29·6·56 | T2J–1 | USN | C | Engineering design of jet trainer | — | — |
| NA–242 | 14·12·55 | F–86K | USAF | LA | 45 sets of airframe assemblies, similar to NA–232 | 45 | — |
| NA–243 | 22·12·55 | F–100F | USAF | LA | Similar to NA–235 | 295 | 243–1 to –295 |
| NA–244 | 5·4·56 | FJ–4B | USN | C | Similar to NA–209, with additional armament | 151 | 244–1 to –151 |
| NA–245 | 8·3·56 | F–100D | USAF | C | Same as NA–224 | 113 | 245–1 to –113 |
| NA–246 | 30·3·56 | UTX | Company | LA | Small jet transport demonstrator (Sabreliner) | 1 | 246–1 |

| CHARGE NUMBER | ORIGINATING DATE | NAME OR DESIGNATION | CUSTOMER | WORKS | DESCRIPTION | QNTY BUILT | CONSTRUCTOR'S NUMBERS |
|---|---|---|---|---|---|---|---|
| NA–247 | 30·4·56 | A3J–1 | USN | C | Production development of NA–233 | 11 | 247–1 to –11 |
| NA–248 | 28·5·56 | FJ–4F | USN | C | Continuation of NA–234 with bipropellant rocket engines | (2) | — |
| NA–249 | 11·7·56 | T2J–1 | USN | C | Production development of NA–241 | 6 | 249–1 to –6 |
| NA–250 | — | — | — | C | Number not assigned | — | — |
| NA–251 | 31·8·56 | FJ–4F | USN | C | Continuation of NA–248, with variable thrust rockets | (2) | — |
| NA–252 | 5·9·56 | T–28C | USN | C | Similar to NA–226 | 56 | 252–1 to –56 |
| NA–253 | 3·10·56 | T2J–1 | USN | C | Continuation of NA–249 production | 121 | 253–1 to –121 |
| NA–254 | 22·3·57 | F–100D | USAF | LA | Contract for 13, similar to NA–235, cancelled 9·9·57 | — | — |
| NA–255 | 22·3·57 | F–100F | USAF | LA | Similar to NA–243 with zero-launch provision | 29 | 255–1 to –29 |
| NA–256 | 23·8·57 | F–86F | USAF | LA | 120 complete airframe sets, as NA–238, for Japan | 120 | — |
| NA–257 | 6·6·57 | F–108 | USAF | LA | Design of long-range interceptor, Weapon System 202A | — | — |
| NA–258 | 3·10·57 | A3J–1 | USN | C | Continuation of NA–233, transferred to NA–247 | — | — |
| NA–259 | 2·1·58 | B–70 | USAF | LA | Phase I development of WS 110A | — | — |
| NA–260 | 22·5·58 | Nomad | Company | C | Modification of one T–28A as civil demonstrator | (1) | — |
| NA–261 | 10·7·58 | F–100F | USAF | LA | Similar to NA–255, for MAP | 9 | 261–1 to –9 |
| NA–262 | 10·12·58 | F–100F | USAF | LA | Similar to NA–255, for MAP | 6 | 262–1 to –6 |
| NA–263 | 26·1·59 | A3J–1 | USN | C | Continuation of NA–247 production | 14 | 263–1 to –14 |
| NA–264 | 31·12·58 | B–70 | USAF | LA | Phase II development of WS 110A, continuation of NA–239 | — | — |
| NA–265 | 2·1·59 | T–39A | USAF | LA | Production variant of NA–246 | 88 | 265–1 to –88 |
| NA–266 | 17·2·59 | T2J–1 | USN | C | Continuation of NA–253 production | 90 | 266–1 to –90 |
| NA–267 | 27·7·59 | B–70 | USAF | LA | Follow-on programme to NA–264 | — | — |
| NA–268 | 11·9·59 | F–108 | USAF | LA | Reserved for Phase II development of NA–257, not used | — | — |
| NA–269 | 16·11·59 | A3J–1 | USN | C | Continuation of NA–263 | 34 | 269–1 to –34 |
|  |  | A3J–2, –3 | USN | C | As above with added fuel, reconnaissance capability | 18 | 269–35 to –52 |
| NA–270 | 16·12·59 | T–39B | USAF | LA | As NA–265 with NASARR | 6 | 270–1 to –6 |
| NA–271 | 21·12·59 | T–39A | USAF | LA | Sabreliner Type certification by FAA | — | — |
| NA–272 | 13·4·60 | A3J–1 | USN | C | Long lead-time effort for seven aircraft, transferred to NA–269 | — | — |
| NA–273 | 28·6·60 | — | US Army | C | Redhead and Roadrunner target missile system | 5 | — |
| NA–274 | 21·9·60 | YB–70 | USAF | LA | Prototype development, follow-on to NA–267 | — | — |
| NA–275 | — | — | — | — | No information | — | — |
| NA–276 | 25·9·61 | T–39A | USAF | LA | Continuation of NA–265 production | 55 | 276–1 to –55 |
| NA–277 | 25·9·61 | T–39D | USN | LA | Similar to NA–270 | 10 | 277–1 to –10 |
| NA–278 | 10·4·61 | XB–70 | USAF | LA | Three prototypes ordered, one cancelled 5·3·64 | 2 | 278–1 and –2 |
| NA–279 | 1·12·61 | RA–5C | USN | C | Continuation of NA–269 production | 20 | 279–1 to –20 |
| NA–280 | 18·1·62 | YT–2B | USN | C | Modification of two T2J–1s to twin-engined configuration | (2) | — |

| CHARGE NUMBER | ORIGINATING DATE | NAME OR DESIGNATION | CUSTOMER | WORKS | DESCRIPTION | QNTY BUILT | CONSTRUCTOR'S NUMBERS |
|---|---|---|---|---|---|---|---|
| NA–281 | — | XB–70 | USAF | LA | Flight test programme for NA–278 first prototype | — | — |
| NA–282 | 16·7·62 | Sabreliner | Remmert-Werner | LA | Commercial production of NA–265 variant | 35 | 282–1 to –35 |
| NA–283 | 2·11·62 | RA–5C | USN | C | Continuation of NA–279 production | 23 | 283–1 to –23 |
| NA–284 | 17·9·62 | YAT–28E | USAF | C | Two T–28A modified with turboprop engines | (2) | 174–324 and 189–57 |
| NA–285 | 16·10·62 | T–39D | USN | LA | Continuation of NA–277 production | 32 | 285–1 to –32 |
| NA–286 | 13·3·63 | XB–70 | USAF | LA | Costs of cancellation of third prototype NA–278 | — | — |
| NA–287 | 13·12·63 | Sabreliner | Company | LA | Specially equipped test-bed for NAA-Autonetics | 1 | 287–1 |
| NA–288 | 7·2·64 | T–2B | USN | C | Production of NA–280 | 10 | 288–1 to –10 |
| NA–289 | 22·5·64 | MQM–42A | US Army | — | Roadrunner target missile | 43 | — |
| NA–290 | 30·6·64 | Sabreliner | Remmert-Werner | LA | Commercial production, as NA–282 | 14 | 282–36 to –49 |
| NA–291 | 22·10·64 | T–2B | USN | C | Continuation of NA–288 production | 36 | 288–11 to –46 |
| NA–292 | 30·11·64 | Sabreliner | Remmert-Werner | LA | Similar to NA–290 | 16 | 282–50 to –65 |
| NA–293 | 27·5·65 | Sabreliner | Remmert-Werner | LA | Similar to NA–292 | 35 | 282–66 to –98 |
| NA–294 | 30·8·65 | T–2B | USN | C | Continuation of NA–291 production | 18 | 294–1 to –18 |
| NA–295 | 12·7·63 | — | — | C | Reserved for USN light attack aircraft, cancelled | — | — |
| NA–296 | 7·4·64 | RA–5C | USN | C | Conversion of A–5A to RA–5C | 27 | — |
| NA–297 | 9·11·65 | Sabreliner | Remmert-Werner | LA | Similar to NA–293 | 25 | 282–99 to –123 |
| NA–298 | 29·12·65 | RA–5C | USN | C | Conversion of A–5A to RA–5C | 16 | — |
| NA–299 | 19·1·66 | Condor | USN | C | Missile development programme | — | — |
| NA–300 | 17·8·64 | OV–10A | USN | C | Development prototypes of light attack aircraft | 7 | 300–1 to –7 |
| NA–301 | 26·8·65 | OV–10A | USN | C | Proposed transport version of NA–300 | — | — |
| NA–302 | 24·1·66 | OV–10A | USN | C | Proposed strike reconnaissance version | — | — |
| NA–303 | 24·1·66 | XB–70 | USAF | LA | Flight test programme, continuation of NA–281 | — | — |
| NA–304 | 7·2·66 | SST | Boeing | LA | Wing pivot test assembly for Boeing SST | — | — |
| NA–305 | 22·5·66 | OV–10A | USN | C | Production of NA–300 for USMC and USAF | 185 | 305–1 to –185 |
| NA–306 | 28·2·66 | Sabreliner 60 | Remmert-Werner | LA | Development and certification of Series 60 version | 2 | 306–1 and –2 |
| NA–307 | 14·3·66 | T–28C | USN | C | Continuation of NA–252 production | 72 | 307–1 to –72 |
| NA–308 | 26·4·66 | Sabreliner 60 | Remmert-Werner | LA | Production of NA–306 | — | 306–3 to –37 |
| NA–309 | 27·5·66 | Condor | USN | C | — | — | — |
| NA–310 | 1·8·66 | T–2B | USN | C | Continuation of NA–294 production (last three, T–2C) | 36 | 310–1 to –36 |
| NA–311 | 2·8·66 | OV–10A | USN | C | Publications and manuals for NA–305 | — | — |
| NA–312 | 3·2·67 | OV–10A | USN | C | Spares and repair parts for NA–305 | — | — |
| NA–318 | — | T–2C | USN | C | Similar to NA–310 with engine change | 48 | 318–1 to –48 |
| NA–332 | — | T–2C | USN | C | Continuation of NA–318 production | 36 | 332–1 to –36 |
| NA–340 | — | T–2C | USN | C | Continuation of NA–332 production | 24 | 340–1 to –24 |
| NR–349 | — | — | USAF | C | Projected A–5C variant for USAF IMI (improved manned interceptor) requirement with three J79 engines | — | — |
| NR–356 | — | — | USN | LA | Projected V/STOL fighter attack aircraft for USN sea control ships | — | — |